Confessions
of a
Stripper

# Confessions of a Stripper

## TALES FROM THE VIP ROOM

by Lacey Lane

HUNTINGTON PRESS

LAS VEGAS, NEVADA

**Confessions of a Stripper—Tales from the VIP Room**

Published by
Huntington Press
3687 South Procyon Avenue
Las Vegas, Nevada 89103
(702) 252-0655 Phone
(702) 252-0675 Fax
e-mail: books@huntingtonpress.com

ISBN 0-929712-92-7

Cover Photo ©Mark Peterson/CORBIS
Cover Design: Bethany Coffey Rihel
Interior Design & Production: Bethany Coffey Rihel

## Dedication

To all the girls baring their bodies
and their souls. Show it while you've got it,
make it while you can, and never
be ashamed of your profession.

# Acknowledgements

I'm indebted to my publisher, Anthony Curtis and Huntington Press, for giving my project a home. To my editor extraordinaire, Deke Castleman, for giving my manuscript clarity and direction. And to my husband, Adam, for giving me love, support, and understanding.

# Contents

# Introduction

My name is Lacey Lane and I take off my clothes for a living. At least, I used to. I retired my g-string awhile back and said goodbye to the stripping scene. During my seven years of topless tenure, I performed at a plethora of strip clubs, bikini bars, and exotic entertainment establishments throughout the country, using more aliases than any ten participants in the federal government's Witness Protection Program. As you can probably imagine, I met thousands of interesting and unusual people along the way—heavy stress on unusual—and the stories I took with me deserve to be chronicled, if only for their entertainment value. Those who have had the pleasure of watching me strut my stuff already got more than their money's worth.

This book is full of outlandish tales from my time in the peek-a-booty biz, but it's more than that. It's a Strip Club 101 of sorts; not only will my accumulated wisdom furnish you with a little extra insight into the world of the topless dancer, but it should help you get more bang for your buck the next time you visit your favorite skin palace. While it's no secret that all you macho hairy-chested testicle owners rule the modern world (although Oprah Winfrey and others are clawing their way into serious contention), when you step inside a strip club, the roles are immediately reversed. Here, the dancers are the hunters and the men are the prey. So trust me when I tell you, you need all the help you can get.

Tales from the VIP Room isn't a scathing tell-all or some tawdry tabloid-esque exposé, so all names and places have been changed to protect the innocent—or the guilty, depending on how you look at it. But don't think for a second that this account is any less accurate or entertaining. Quite the contrary, actually. Omitting true identities has actually afforded me the literary freedom to serve you my memories on the half-shell. In essence, raw and untainted.

Somewhere between inanimate smut magazines and full-service prostitution is the niche occupied by strip clubs. This fascinating industry, an equal mixture of endless fantasy and hardcore reality, is different for all those involved in it—be it for business or pleasure. For me, it was a combination of both. And so, without further ado, I give you Confessions of a Stripper: Tales from the VIP Room. Enjoy!

# Part One

## Confessions of a Stripper

# 1

# Welcome to the Show

A close friend of mine once said that there are more strip clubs in America than Chinese restaurants. I believe he's correct. But as you might expect, no two are alike.

Some strip clubs are posh megabuck establishments routinely frequented by superstar athletes and major celebrities from the music, television, and film worlds. Other clubs are sleazy skankfests, little more than fronts for nickel-and-dime prostitution, which appeal to the minimum-wage set. Some are architectural marvels with elaborate décor. Others seem to have been thrown together overnight, haphazardly furnished courtesy of a bargain-basement yard sale. Some have world-class menus with cuisine that rivals four- and five-star restaurants. Others serve grub far beneath the standards of what you'd expect to find at a decrepit service station along a seldom-used roadway. Some are chock full of beautiful and talented dancers, women you could easily find on the pages of Playboy and Penthouse. Others offer up scary-looking hags who conjure up spells and ride on broomsticks. But regardless of their differences, all strip clubs have at least one thing in common: They're recognized throughout the world by men (and women) as locales where fantasies can be indulged, legally.

Every now and then, a strip club comes under fire for some violation or another—owners and employees have been indicted for everything from drugs and prostitution to racketeering and extortion—but for the most part, the laws are obeyed and the clubs remain in business. Legal issues aside, the people who work at the strip clubs have been branded by many as perverted and loathsome denizens of debauchery. The truth is, those descriptions can be appropriately applied to anyone—from jobless vagrants to members of Congress and everyone in between. It simply depends on the specific individual. At one point, William Jefferson Clinton was said to be perverted, loathsome, and debauched, along with a host of even more critical adjectives, and at the time he was the leader of the free world!

Prior to my submersion into the world of topless dancing, I, too, bought into the "badge of dishonor" stigma that most strippers and their associates are forced to wear. But my ignorance quickly gave way to enlightenment when I saw with my own eyes what really happens on the inside. Still, certain generalizations surrounding the positions within the topless industry, and the people who fill them, are strangely accurate. And due to these consistencies, I often wondered if there were established criteria for a club's personnel.

For example, strip club managers almost always seem to fit that Guido-esque image: Tony Soprano wanna-bes long before The Sopranos hit the small screen. Maybe it's the aura of power and respect that goes hand in hand with those who are, or claim to be, mobbed-up, but whatever the reasoning, I was amazed by how many club bosses shared the modern gangster persona. One club manager who was as Italian as Woody Allen went so far as to speak with an obviously adopted "fuhgeddaboudit" lilt and came off sounding like a bad version of a Budweiser commercial.

Those club managers who didn't play at being wiseguys usually looked as if they belonged in a circus sideshow. With elaborate tattoos that would make sci-fi animators envious, eyebrow and lip piercings that caused problems with airport security, and a dress code that Marilyn Manson would shy away from, these creatures of the night would never be found in the boardroom of a Fortune 500 company—unless they were there to collect a tab that some executive flaked out on. Ironically, some of the sweetest strip club managers in the business, those I dealt with, at any rate, are of the freak-show variety.

Generally speaking, a club's clientele determines what the owner/manager looks like. If there are a lot of expensive cars in the valet lot, I'd bet a week's worth of tips that the man making the decisions wears a loose-fitting gold watch and a thick gold chain around his neck with some kind of oversized gaudy pendant. Also, his thinning hair is probably slicked back and he perpetually chomps on a $20 cigar. However, show me a club with a "Nude Girls" sign out front and a self-parking lot filled with beater cars and broken bottles, and 99 times out of 100 the boss is someone who always looks like he's dressed for Halloween.

When it comes to bartenders, the strip clubs certainly get their fair share of characters. The majority of those I encountered were always yammering about some elaborate get-rich-quick scheme, usually involving real estate, and when they finally made it, they'd come back and take me away from all this, as if I were some damsel in distress needing to be rescued. Bartenders across the board are known for constantly perusing the Help Wanted ads, looking for better gigs. Strip club drink-slingers are no exception, except there's just as good a chance that they're looking in the sports section for a spread on an upcoming game; most of the bartenders I knew were always betting on something. And every bartender had his special little trick, a well-rehearsed move he performed for you right before asking you out, thinking that it would improve his chances of getting the date. Over the years, I witnessed many. One had a bottle-juggling routine that would have put the antics in Cocktail to shame. Another regaled you with obscure facts, a la the mailman from Cheers, while mixing your drink. But the best was the bartender who doused his thumb with grenadine, then lit it on fire so he could showily light your cigarette. If I remember correctly, he was missing part of an eyebrow! Those guys would use the same moves—and the same pick-up lines—on all the dancers. For the record, I never dated a mixologist from a club I was working at. From my experience, bartenders were the biggest "trophy-date" hunters out there, far worse than the customers. And they weren't even paying for the privilege!

Bouncers—notoriously big and dumb—were always complaining about that one major injury that kept them from reaching the pros. I'm sad to say it, but in all my ass-shaking years, not once did I meet a doorman who could carry on a meaningful conversation for more than a few minutes. Too bad, really, because many of those guys were major hunks—chiseled facial features with bodies to match. A shame that they had the intelligence of lampposts. That's not to say their imposing size and strength weren't greatly appreciated. Dancers depend on the presence of these dim-wit gorillas to keep them safe. Every now and then a customer (usually a drunk) gets unruly and an example has to be made. You don't guard Fort Knox with water pistols. Well, the dancers are a strip club's gold bars and keeping them safe requires an effective means of protection.

Only once did I go out on a date with a bouncer I worked

with. He had asked me out a few times, but I'd always turned him down. It's not that I wasn't attracted to him—I was—but I didn't like mixing work and play. However, he was persistent and I eventually caved in. Big mistake.

He took me to a prime rib buffet, my first indication that it was going to be my last date with him. Not that I'm some prissy missy, but I could have thought of a zillion other places for a solid first impression instead of a $9.99 all-you-can-eat heart disease festival where every patron looked like a stand-in for the Hindenburg.

After watching him devour approximately half a cow (I almost became a vegetarian that night), which he washed down with what seemed like an entire keg of beer, and listening to his endless tales of playing football for a major college in the Midwest and how he should have been drafted in the first round except for some kind of problem with his back, not to mention his falling out with the coaching staff, he suggested we go back to his place to catch the end of the Monday Night Football game and get to know each other better. I quickly chimed in with a better plan: Take me home immediately and never ask me out again.

Finally, there are the dancers, the most important people in any strip club. Without mincing words, dancers always have drama in their lives. I was no exception. But given the nature of the profession, it would be hard to imagine it any other way. Regardless of what you think or what you know or what you think you know, earning a living as an exotic dancer (regardless of how exotic you really are) is no easy mission. It's hard on the body and hard on the mind, even if you have no problem with showing yourself off to total strangers. When working, dancers are required to always be "on," like an actor or actress filming a five-hour scene (or longer) without interruption. Ask any of the most respected thespians on the planet and I'm sure they'd agree—such a task would be nearly impossible to pull off, let alone to do effectively. Yet this is precisely what a stripper does on a nightly basis.

There are many reasons women gravitate toward this profession: the lure of big money; the prospect of meeting wealthy men; because they are exhibitionistic in nature; or simply because they can't see themselves settling into the drudgery of a traditional nine-to-five job. Whatever their reasons, and the varying backgrounds from which they hail, it's easy to imagine how a few nights a week of portraying flesh-and-blood visual sex toys for what literally amounts to an audience of wallets with heartbeats could create some tension. Perhaps that's why the turnover rate is so high and why women come and go from the different clubs—and the profession itself—like addicted gamblers from an OTB. Bottom line, it's a tremendously difficult profession, but one that can be extremely rewarding—for the right individuals.

It certainly was for me.

# 2

# The Psyche of a Topless Dancer

To truly understand the world of topless dancing and all it entails, you first need to understand—or *attempt* to understand—the dancers, themselves. I touched on this briefly in the Introduction, but I have no qualms about stating it again: The strippers are the very core of the exotic entertainment business. Without them, the tassels just won't twirl. Obviously, like the clubs they perform in, no two dancers are ever completely alike. But one commonality shared by the overwhelming majority is their love of money. "Greed is good" is how Gordon Gekko (Michael Douglas in *Wall Street*) summed it up. In today's MTV-inspired lingo, "Dollar dollar bill y'all" would be the slang translation. Regardless of how it's conveyed, the message is the same and cold hard cash was the sole reason I shook my tight toned ass and firm (at that point, natural) boobs at every Tom, Dick, and Harry (and occasionally Jane) four to five nights a week for the better part of seven years.

Although it didn't start out that way.

Not even close.

Growing up, I had a severe problem with self-esteem. I was extremely attractive. I had a killer body and tons of friends. And I never once had difficulty getting a date. Forgive my egotistical self-touting, but I had to beat the guys off with a stick. However, self-doubt absolutely consumed me. I had a terrible time making decisions, believing whichever choice I made would be the wrong one, so I opted to have someone else take the reins. I worried a lot, too, about anything and everything. Like chronic depression or some form of addiction, it wasn't something I could control. For example, I worried about getting bad grades in school, which would get me into trouble at home. Of course, I never did receive those bad grades, but the knots in my stomach were always present, ready to constrict at a moment's notice. I was also plagued by separation anxiety, but that has just as much to do with being a twin as it does with what I believe is the root of my evils: my abandonment issues.

My mother and father divorced when I was two years old. Six months later he remarried—a woman with two children. Instant family, just add *my* father. His new family consumed him and, for all intents and purposes, we were completely forgotten. Child-support payments were also forgotten. It was as if to him, we'd never existed. Over the next 11 months, wherever my mother went, my sister and I went with her. The grocery store, the dentist, the *bathroom*, you name it—we were both total cling-ons. But then my mother started dating again, leaving the house for hours and days at a time, and my feelings of loss and abandonment began to manifest. Now, it wasn't as if my sister and I were left alone in some dark decrepit basement without food or water. Quite the contrary. We were living with my grandparents at the time, in a luxurious house on Long Island, chock full of maids and attendants, ready to wait on us hand and foot. But that didn't affect my yearning or quell my feelings of being left behind. Many times I woke up in the middle of the night and went to the stairs or the front door to wait for my mother to return, and that's where someone would find me in the morning, asleep on the floor.

This went on for the better part of seven years until my mom remarried. That union effected a new emotion in me, one that came from deep within—anger. I had always been the sweet one, a total Pollyanna, always looking for and finding the best in any situation. But my new stepfather was a harsh taskmaster, not to mention extremely over-protective. So over-protective, in fact, that leaving the house was impossible. My friends had to come up with ingenious ways to smuggle me out. Authority had been passed to my stepfather and it infuriated me that he was now the disciplinarian. One incident in specific I will take with me to the grave. My stepfather found a few small pieces of a Devil Dog dessert treat on the carpeted stairs. He gathered my two sisters and me to find out who the culprit was. When no one confessed, he snatched up the crumbs and angrily rubbed them into our hair. But despite his overbearing nature and cruel disciplinary tactics, my stepfather had a very strong work ethic. Early on, he taught me the value of money, although putting me to work at the age of 13 (after-school jobs at grocery and ice-cream stores) to help contribute was a bit much. It's not like we were even close to being poor or destitute.

Throughout my high school years, I didn't think about my real father at all, although I'm relatively certain that the ease with which he erased me from his memory contributed largely to my self-esteem issues, issues that were like rusty daggers in my side. I knew I had to do something to overcome them—otherwise they would most assuredly overcome me, to the point that I wouldn't be able to function normally. What exactly does that mean? I couldn't really tell you. Would I crawl under my covers and wait to die? Would I go on an eating binge and balloon to 900 pounds? Would

I put a gun to my head and pull the trigger? Who knows? At the time, I certainly didn't.

I read a few books on depression, thinking they might help me to work out the issues for myself. From them, I took comfort in the fact that other girls (and boys) out there had the same feelings I did, and that helped me to feel less like an outcast, but they didn't do a damn thing to "cure" me. A shrink was also on tap, but for $250 an hour he just regurgitated things that I had told him and suggested possible roots for my issues, the majority relating to my father and stepfather. No duh, Doc! A stranger on a bus could have told me as much—and saved me $249 in the process. What I desperately needed to know was how to make those feelings go away. And as the years passed, I realized it was something I would have to do for myself. Sadly, I wasn't getting any closer to an answer.

One night, during my sophomore year in college, a bunch of my guy friends decided to go to a strip joint and asked me to come along. I'd never been to a strip club before—in my mind, they were reserved for drunken bachelor parties or horny old men who never got to see live naked women unless they paid for the privilege. On top of that, the thought of a woman—and not just any woman, *me!*—going to one of those lewd dens of iniquity was a completely alien concept. Understand, I wasn't prudish, or prissy, or stuck-up. I just had old-fashioned views on sex. Some of my girlfriends were real boy-toys, piling up one-night stands like they were designer outfits on closeout sales. I, on the other hand, was always relationship-minded and monogamous; for that reason, I didn't lose my virginity until I was 18. It was the most sacred thing I owned (next to my Trans Am) and I wasn't about to let anyone get a free ride until I was plenty good and ready to have a passenger.

But whether I wanted to admit it or not, I had always secretly wondered what really happened inside one of those places. I had heard so many stories that I often wondered what was fiction and what was fact. And now that I had the opportunity to find out for myself once and for all, I was not about to let it pass.

On a scale of Phyllis Diller to Marilyn Monroe, the strip club we went to that night rated a solid Carmen Electra—what I would consider the perfect combination of sleazy and sexy. The guys each paid a cover charge of $10, a bargain when you consider what they got to see. My admission was free, but the gorilla-like doorman's reptilian stare-and-smile combo made me feel as if I'd paid the full fare—with my soul.

Inside, the set-up was impressive. I'd been in numerous bars before, but nothing like this. There was a large, sweeping, ebony-colored bar off to the right with about 20 stools, thickly cushioned oversized booths around the room's perimeter that looked as if they could seat six adults comfortably, and a host of two-, four-, and six-top tables. Three stages dominated the room. The two flanking the main stage were smaller by about a third and each had a gleaming silver pole—like the kind you'd find in a firehouse—running from floor to ceiling. The main stage jutted farther into the room than the two pole-stages and was connected to what I presumed was the dressing room by a narrow disco-light catwalk seemingly right out of *Dance Fever*. To the left of the catwalk was the source of the sounds: a raised glass-encased DJ booth. The entire club was bathed in an orange-amber glow that reminded me of a snifter of Grand Marnier. It's too bad the club didn't smell as appealing—just a sweet-and-sour commingling of cheap perfume, cigarette smoke, and sweat. But there was an additional aroma in the room, an overpowering bouquet common to casinos, card rooms, and racetracks. Now that I really think about it, perhaps it was more of an aura than an actual smell. I'm talking, of course, about money.

At the moment we entered the club, the pole stages were empty. All eyes were locked in rapt attention on the main stage where two centerfold-quality blondes, naked except for their colored-dental-floss thongs, were smearing each other with iridescent body paint. Under the many pin-spot black lights, which were trained on the girls like snipers' sighting lasers, the body paint reacted like the skin of chameleons walking across a Twister board.

My guy friends whooped, hollered, and high-fived each other, as if their favorite football team had just won the Super Bowl, before making beelines for an open table not far from the stage, leaving me behind as if I were nothing more than a rusty car part on the side of the road. But it wouldn't have mattered. I don't think I could have followed them under my own power if I had wanted to. I was actually frozen in place, assaulted by a mixture of emotions: shock, fascination, and embarrassment.

Shock: Two women were doing this in public!

Fascination: Two women were doing this in public!

Embarrassment: Two women were doing this in public and, based on my initial visual recon of the room, besides the dancers and the cocktail waitresses I was the only other woman in the place!

Eventually, my legs thawed and I was able to walk to the table my buddies had selected. With the two dancers now bent over, butt cheek to butt cheek, grabbing their ankles and coating each other's buns with the funky fingerpaint, I could tell that my friends, along with every other hot-and-bothered male in the place, were envisioning a quarterback-and-center scenario unlike any you'd ever see on Monday Night Football.

After another 30 seconds, the lather-fest ended. The two girls were showered with applause and whistles, not to mention swarms of tossed, handed, and tucked bills. It took the two of them nearly ten minutes to snatch, pluck, and scoop all the greenbacks that came their way. It was at that moment that a new emotion forced its way into my consciousness: awe.

Standing on the raised platform before me were two five-foot-nothing featherweight girls, seemingly not much older than I was, and they had every swinging dick in the place basically licking their boots. (I'm sure that, had one of the girls actually been wearing boots, she would have had plenty of volunteers to tongue-scrub them 'til they shined!) Even my friends, muscle-bound tough guys who played football for a major Division I school, were reduced to the equivalent of gelatinous masses in a matter of seconds. Wow! Had I not seen it for myself, I wouldn't have believed it. But the proof was right there in front of me—and they were still raking in their dough.

It was truly empowering. I felt proud to be a woman. My thoughts momentarily turned to my Political Science 101 class where, a few days before, we had briefly discussed the Equal Rights Amendment. Eyes locked on the strippers, I thought that it was a crying shame America's political process wasn't based solely on the happenings inside a strip club. If that were the case, the balance of power in this country would be vastly different.

As I watched the girls fetch the last of their cash, I started wondering what kind of iron constitution was required to step out on stage and let it all hang out—literally—in front of what amounted to a pack of hungry lions. I was certain that not one single woman who performed in a strip club thought of herself as ugly or worthless. Perhaps this was the solution to my self-esteem problem. A far stretch, I admitted to myself, but if I could somehow work in a place like this, maybe I would subconsciously break free of the issues that were hampering me—issues I didn't even have a handle on. Unfortunately, while it sounded like a reasonable consideration, the thought opened a fresh can of worms.

The problem: There wasn't a snowball's chance in hell that I would shed my clothes for money. I didn't care what they paid me. I didn't have a problem with my body—at least, not one that I *knew* of—but that didn't mean I wanted to show it off to total strangers. However, I did have some experience as a waitress. Maybe if I could get a job cocktailing in such a sex-crazed atmosphere, wearing one of the skimpy outfits the drink-chicks wore—fuck-me pumps, a barely there skirt, and a bikini top that left nothing to the imagination— maybe that would be enough to get me over the hump (a fitting word considering we're talking about the sex industry). At the very least, I figured that by delivering drinks dressed like a call girl I'd be able to put some cash into my pocket instead of shelling it out to a psychiatrist.

The more I thought about it, the more I liked the idea. So while my friends got their dollar bills ready for the next show on stage, I sought out the club's manager. The bartender pointed him out to me and I immediately wished he hadn't. Growing up, my younger sister was a huge fan of professional wrestling. Well, this guy was the spitting image of greasy manager Lou Albano, complete with a red rubberband around his pubic hair-like goatee. How this guy thought he looked good was beyond me. Think of a short fat dildo with hair. Anyway, had he not been looking directly at me when the bartender pointed him out, I would have gone back to the table where my friends were in a heartbeat. I mean, this guy *really* creeped me out!

But it was too late, so I took a deep breath, mustered all the courage I could, and walked up to him. Respectfully, and trying to be professional, I reached out to shake his hand. He took my hand in his, brought it to his lips, and kissed it. Not like a gentlemen would, mind you, but openmouthed, making certain I felt his hot slimy tongue on my knuckles. When he pulled his mouth away, a filmy strand of saliva remained connected for a few moments before snapping. I thought I was going to vomit. Somehow, I choked down the nausea building up inside me and was about to pop the question when he beat me to the punch.

"Lemme guess, sweetie," he said, talking to my tits. "You wanna work here?"

"Was I that obvious?" I replied, unsure of how else to respond.

"Every girl who comes in here wants to be one of *my* girls," he bragged. The way he said it was reason enough for me to look elsewhere for my therapy, but I knew that dealing with a scum-sucking pig like him was, in all likelihood, part of the process that might ultimately cure my mental ailment. So I stayed put.

"Are there any openings?" I asked.

"Funny," he said with a grotesque smirk. "I was gonna ask you the same thing."

I looked at him curiously, as if I didn't understand the comment. But inside my mind, I was kicking him in the nuts repeatedly with a steel-toed boot.

After nearly half a minute of awkward silence, he asked: "Got any drug problems or felonies?"

I shook my head, no.

"Any jealous boyfriends I might have to throw out of here?"

Once again, a shake of the head did the talking.

"What kind of dancing experience do you have?"

I smiled. "I don't want to dance," I said. "I want to be a cocktail waitress."

It was his turn to shake his head. "Don't need any drink-schleppers, honey. What I need is dancers. And you look like you'd do real well …" Once again, he addressed my chest: "Assuming your body looks as good *out* of clothes as it does in them."

I blushed and thanked him for the, uh, compliment, but explained that I had never danced in a topless club before and that I had no desire to show more skin than the cocktail waitresses did.

He shrugged, then threw up his hands. "Then I can't help you," he said coldly. "Try Denny's. They're always looking for waitresses."

Dejected but relieved that I wouldn't have an Albano-clone for a boss, I started to walk away—but he stopped me with a firm hand on my shoulder and spun me around. "You really should give dancing some thought." He gave another sick grimace. "If not for your benefit, for mine."

I didn't respond verbally, although I wanted to. In the worst way! Instead I pulled away and went back to my friends' table. When I arrived, a tall pretty redhead with a billion freckles, small boobs, and a big ass was giving them a table dance. Excited by my return, the guys thrust me into a chair and had the stripper dance for me. My cheeks turned brighter than her hair, but I saw that all my buddies were getting into it, so I sat there, let the girl do her thing, and let the guys get their money's worth.

I watched closely as she gyrated and swiveled around me. I got the feeling she had somehow detached herself from the action. She simply treated the table dance as a chore for which she got paid.

When the dance was over, the stripper collected her fee and tip, then moved on to another table. My friends all high-fived me and asked me if it was as good for me as it was for them. They said other things, too, all on the subject of threesomes. It started out funny, but after a while my earlier nausea returned. I like one-on-one affairs, with men only. Not that I have a problem with homosexuality, but I've always preferred the company of a man.

After I'd had enough of the sailor talk, I excused myself to go to the ladies' room. When I came out, I saw the red-headed stripper sitting just a few feet away at a small table by herself, sipping a glass of wine. I walked over and asked if

I could join her for a moment. Although she wasn't as con-genial as before—when money was involved—she nodded and motioned for me to sit.

"You're a good dancer," I said, more as an icebreaker than a compliment. In truth, I thought her dancing abil-ity—at least, what I had observed—was about average. Paula Abdul, she wasn't. "How long have you been stripping?"

She took a sip of wine. "Three years, on and off."

"How do you do it? Where do you find the courage?"

"I've got two kids to feed," she stated matter-of-factly. "And an ex-husband who wouldn't know child support from fairy dust. This puts food in their mouths, clothes on their backs and still gives me plenty of quality time with them."

I was impressed. Here she was, a single mother, grab-bing the bull by the horns and providing for her kids the best she could. This was hard work. I started thinking of her as a good role model for women. Looking at her more closely, I could tell she didn't live a pampered life. Makeup, even the excessive amount she used, can only hide so much.

"Do you ever get nervous when you dance?"

"When I started I was scared shitless," she said. "But I got drunk a lot during my first few months, which really helped." Okay, so much for the role model. "Now I look at it like it's just another job. Same as working in a restaurant or behind a sales counter. Trust me, I did both. They're bor-ing and the pay is lousy."

Well, she was right on both counts. I, too, had worked as a waitress and at a cosmetics counter. Boring? Big time. Lousy pay? You betcha.

"You're thinking about giving it a try, huh?"

"I'm thinking about it," I said. "Don't know if I'm cut out for it, though."

"Some girls are, some girls aren't," she said and drained the rest of her wine. She stood up, then looked me square in the eyes. "But if you come to work here, just stay the hell out of my way. I've got enough competition as it is." She walked away without another word.

O-kay. However, I took her statement as a compliment. If she felt I would be competition, that had to be a good thing, didn't it?

Based on what I'd seen and what I knew about women in general, it wasn't hard to picture the business of exotic dancing as ultra-competitive, where dancers fought with each other tooth and nail for the wealthiest best-tipping customers. In fact, it was impossible to imagine it as anything else. Think about it. Women are catty enough as it is when it comes to their looks, bodies, and outfits. But throw money into the mix, in an industry that I guessed would be largely visual-dependent, and it wasn't hard to envision a continuous World War III. While working in a topless club might be just what the doctor ordered for my beleaguered self-image, that method of treatment could very well lead to other ailments—for example, a bleeding ulcer, or a broken nose if I happened to get on Ms. Pale-n-Pasty Redhead's bad side, which I might already have accomplished.

After another hour, we left the club. The guys were flat broke, dead drunk, and hornier than rabbits on Viagra. On the way home, with me at the wheel, I suggested they seek out some freshmen football groupies, the kind of girls who would even screw the kicker just to say they'd made it with a member of the team. Either that or hit the showers. *Cold* showers. All I know is, as soon as I parked the car, I got the hell out of Dodge. Sure, they were my friends, but remaining in the company of four seriously drunk and horny guys, all of whom weighed 230-plus, after they'd spent the better part of the evening at a strip club would not have been an intelligent move on my part.

That night, I gave the idea of working as a topless dancer a lot of serious deliberation. It was something I'd never even considered before—not even remotely—but the thought of potentially working out some problems and making some decent money along the way certainly had its merits. I began to envision all the fantastic things I would buy myself—after my student loans were paid off, of course. The more I considered it, the more it seemed like a good idea (bleeding ulcers and broken noses aside). But I still wasn't wholly convinced. So I decided to do some more research.

# 3

# Look and Learn

Over the next week and a half, I visited eight different strip clubs, all within 40 miles of my apartment. Not once did I have to pay a cover charge. I dressed down for my research, trying not to attract too much attention. After all, I was there only to pick up tidbits of information, not to get picked up by anyone. After a quick perusal of an establishment, I would order a drink at the bar, then slink off to a back table, trying to blend into the shadows where I could watch the action without being disturbed. In most cases, no one bothered me—the gloomier the lighting, the easier it was to remain anonymous. Occasionally, a dancer sought me out and hit me up for a lap dance. A few times I indulged—for research purposes only.

After one lap dance, the stripper asked me for my phone number. I guess she figured if I was there, alone, I had to be trolling for a companion. I turned her down politely, telling her that I was flattered, but already involved. She scribbled her number on the drink napkin with my lipstick and told me to call her if I changed my mind. I remember spitting my gum into the napkin later that night.

In regard to the lap dances, they provided me with a host of up-close-and-personal visuals. Though a few were a tad unsettling, the girls unknowingly gave me some excellent pointers. I filed them away as I noticed them (more on these later) and went on with my research.

At one club, I was pestered constantly—this time, by customers. The men must have felt that any woman at a strip club who didn't work there must either be easy or bisexual or (lucky them!) both. I was neither and I turned them down like a counterfeit bill at a casino cage. It was at this club that I had my first experience with the inside of a VIP Room.

I was looking for the bathroom. At the back of the club was a long hallway lined with doors. Strangely, they were marked with silver numbers and each had a small colored lightbulb above it. I assumed they were like airplane lavatories, the light bulbs indicating whether or not they were occupied. The first few doors were closed and the bulbs above them were on. Farther down the hall, I found one door that was ajar, the bulb above it out, so I went inside. Surprisingly, there was no toilet or sink, but wall-to-wall mirrors and two oversized pastel loveseats, arranged caddy-corner. Both looked as if they belonged on the set of the old "Miami Vice" TV show. A small glass cocktail table completed the furnishings. Realizing my mistake, I turned around to leave—just as two dancers were entering, leading two male customers by their hands.

I apologized for being in their way and tried to squeeze by, but the guys wouldn't have any of it. Mid-40s, deeply tanned and dressed in expensive suits, they weren't the most handsome of individuals, but you could tell they had money. In fact, they exuded cash. I'd seen a few flashy exotic cars in the parking lot—in the roped-off valet section—when I entered the club and I wouldn't have been surprised if these two players were the owners. Rather than seem annoyed by my presence, both men quickly invited me to stay. However, it was painfully obvious that the two dancers didn't share their sentiments. Out of the corner of my eye, I caught the strippers flashing each other angry looks—but I knew the experience would be too good to pass up, regardless of any animosity it may have caused. Turning on the charm, I grabbed both men by the arms and told them I'd be delighted. My pee-pee break would just have to wait.

We remained in the VIP Room for a few drinks and a total of six songs. Apparently, in these back rooms, much closer contact between dancer and customer was allowed. Either that, or the strippers were seriously committed to upstaging my presence. But I noticed it was always the dancers who initiated the contact. Guys had to stay put and keep their hands to themselves. At least, that's how it was in theory (but more on that later).

That night, one of the girls really went over the line, thrusting every part of her body in both of the guys' faces. At one point, she even climbed up on the loveseats, pulled her G-string aside and rubbed her bare coochie against their foreheads. Nasty! The guys didn't seem to mind, however. I was pretty sickened by what I saw and wished to God I'd passed on the backroom invite. On the other hand, I was glad to have been present for the labia tango. If that's what girls commonly did in the VIP Rooms, I wanted no part of it.

During the songs, I carried on polite small talk with the guys, but all three of us were more interested in the dancers' antics—them for their reasons and me for mine. When the last song was over, the guys paid up—$200 apiece for the dances, plus a $100 tip for each. I couldn't believe my eyes. In less than 30 minutes, each of those girls had made $300! I was mesmerized by the quick cash, but the brief episode of extreme contact still had me wondering.

On the way out of the room, the guys asked me for my number. Not wanting to appear ungrateful for the drinks and, uh, entertainment, I shelled out a phone number—but it definitely wasn't mine. We said our goodbyes in the hallway and the guys walked off. However, the two girls blockaded me before I could enter back into the club. Oh shit, I thought, here it comes. I was certain that I was about to get my ass kicked by two jealous topless dancers. But rather than start a fight or curse me out, they *thanked* me. They admitted that, at the beginning of the session, they absolutely hated the idea of me being back there with them, fearing it was going to cut into their tips. But as it turned out, both strippers believed that my presence kept them from having to fend off the guys' overly aggressive advances.

Bunny, a brunette, the taller of the two girls, said they'd danced for those two guys numerous times before. Apparently, each time it was the same—a six-song session for $300. But on all the other occasions—more than a dozen—both men were extremely handsy. This time, other than for a few minor pets and pats, they were perfect gentlemen.

Nikki, the shorter dancer with the bigger boobs, went so far as to invite me for a cup of coffee. She said she and Bunny were done for the night—thanks to the last two guys, they had each cleared the $800 mark. Not too shabby for a night's work. Hoping to fill in the blanks for some, if not all, of my remaining questions about the exotic entertainment industry, I readily accepted.

The girls changed and we went to a nearby coffeehouse. For the first 15 minutes of our cappuccino and conversation, I thought Bunny and Nikki might be lesbians looking for a third chica to add to their fluff-party. But as the evening progressed, I learned that wasn't the case at all; these two were actually just nice girls—a rarity, I later discovered, in the topless biz.

First, they confessed their real names. Nikki—5'2", 101

aerobics-toned pounds with big firm boobs that she said were natural—was really Jennifer, a student at a nearby community college. In her mid-20s, she'd been dancing for 18 months. Bunny, the tall "coochie rubber" with the body of a ballerina, was actually Rebecca. She'd been dancing for nine years and had turned 32 three weeks prior. She owned her car outright—a sporty red BMW convertible—and had just put a sizable down payment on a house, all courtesy of her tits and ass, and the men who paid to see them.

For Rebecca, the profession was a by-product of what she really wanted to do—become a theatrical dancer on Broadway. She'd studied for years to achieve her dream, but chronic knee problems, and two surgeries, eventually caused her to abandon the chase. Unable to get dancing completely out of her system, Rebecca began working as a dancer in a bikini bar, but when a friend told her how much money she was making at a full-fledged topless joint, Rebecca quickly made the switch.

"As you can see, I'm pretty flat up top," Rebecca said. "Showing them off isn't that big of a deal."

That's when I questioned her about the baring of her privates. Even Jennifer was curious about that maneuver. Rebecca laughed, putting her head in her hands.

"I've never done anything like that before," she said with a giggle. "But tonight I had two really good reasons. First, I wanted to completely skeeve you out." I told her she definitely had. "But the second and real reason I did it was because I had the worst itch on the edge of my pussy lip."

Both Jennifer and I broke up laughing, nearly spitting up our lattés in the process. When we got our breath back, I asked Jennifer how she got started in the topless biz. Her answer totally blew me away.

"I was super shy all through high school. Never even had a date until the prom, and even then, I went with my cousin. I was geeky-looking, too. Big framed glasses, braces, bad skin … the works. Needless to say, my self-image sucked. Then one night I saw a movie and it had a scene with top-less dancers in it, with tons of guys fighting for their atten-tion, and it really stuck in my mind. So the next semester, I skipped the regular classes and registered for two dance classes, an aerobics class and a martial-arts class. I was deter-mined to get in shape and learn some moves—moves that would help me while I was dancing and help me if some guy acted up and I needed to kick the shit out of him. Any-way, at the end of the semester, I felt great, looked even better, and figured it was now or never. So I went to the club, danced for the boss, and he hired me on the spot."

When she finished her story, I had tears in my eyes. I shared with them my own issues and told them what I was thinking about doing to rectify the situation.

"You're definitely not alone," Jennifer said. "When I started, I thought I was the only one with a confidence prob-lem. Even though they won't admit it—heck, most of the girls won't even *talk* to you, let alone share their innermost feelings—the majority of the dancers out there have prob-lems with self-esteem."

"It kind of comes with the territory," Rebecca added.

"Too fat, too skinny, boobs too small, teeth not straight enough, smile not white enough, ass too big … You name it, it's always something, whether it's true or not."

"But you don't seem to have any problems like that," I said.

Rebecca made a show of pretending to be a stuck-up snob, haughty accent and all. "Yes, well," she began, flip-ping her hair back and her nose in the air, "I'm just perfect in every respect."

We got a good laugh over that one. And then, rather than try to steer me away from the stripping business for fear I would horn in on their customers and their tips, they encouraged me to go for it. What's more, they told me to come work at *their* club. In fact, they insisted, telling me I would really disappoint them if I didn't.

"But isn't it horribly competitive?" I asked. "I mean, girls fighting for the same customers?"

"When it comes to regular customers, especially VIP Roomers with fat bankrolls, yes," Rebecca concurred. "Then, it's every girl for herself. And even beyond that, you'll find that most of the dancers are total cunts. Truth is, there are plenty of guys and plenty of money. And a guy knows what kind of woman he wants to dance for him the second he sees her. I don't care what any of the other girls say, but some nights it's the girl with the big boobs and the perfect body who makes all the money and other nights it's the nastiest fattest cow in the place that breaks the bank. Most of the girls who try to make it competitive are lazy obnoxious bitches who find something to complain about no matter what the situation. Sure, there are exceptions, and a lot of girls social-ize with each other because they have to, working conditions and all, but in most cases they just don't like each other."

"Beca's right," Jennifer said. "And there's only one way to deal with girls like that."

"How?"

"Put Visine in their drinks," she replied matter-of-factly.

Rebbeca laughed and made a face, as if recalling some previous event. But I was clueless. "Why, what's that do?" I queried.

"Have you ever seen someone with explosive diarrhea?" Jennifer asked. "If not, I have only two words for you: Stand back."

Rebecca's laugh grew louder. Jennifer joined her. Even I was laughing and I had no clue why. Toilet humor usually doesn't appeal to me, but the two of them were so infectious I couldn't help myself.

"Visine really does that?" I asked. "How'd you learn about it?"

"Jen's dad is a high-school science teacher," Rebecca said. "I didn't believe her—until I saw the results first-hand."

"Oh my God," I said. "You actually did it to another dancer?"

"Nope," Jennifer said with a giggle. "One of the bouncers. Fucking asshole pinched my ass every time I walked by him, which was like fifty times a night. He did it so many times I had a bruise the size of a golf ball."

"Not good for business at all," Rebecca said. "Even a big ass is better than a bruised ass. Guys dig scars and tattoos, but for some reason a bruise has the same effect as a mass of pimples."

Just the thought of it nearly made me gag. "So what happened to the bouncer?" I asked, now more than a bit curious.

"He came in on his night off," Jennifer continued. "Pinched my ass four or five times within twenty minutes. That was it. I was gonna get that big black motherfucker and I let him know it, too. Well, I was just coming down from my turn on stage and I headed to the bar for a drink when I saw JT heading off to the bathroom. But the stupid ox left his bottle of beer unprotected. So when the bartender wasn't looking, I grabbed the Visine out of my purse, which I keep behind the bar for cigarette breaks, and squeezed in a ton of drops. Good thing JT was already pretty drunk or else he might have tasted it. Anyway, about fifteen minutes later there was a commotion up at the bar. When I got there, I wished I hadn't."

"Shit everywhere," Rebecca chimed in. "Stunk to high heaven, too. I heard JT had been to some all-you-can-eat sushi buffet before he got to the club. By the looks of what was on the floor, he got his money's worth. I guarantee you one thing, that sonofabitch will never leave the house without underwear on again."

Jennifer and I both got nauseous. I was about to take a sip of my coffee, but I set the mug down. Now I didn't even want to look at the brownish-black liquid, let alone put it in my mouth.

Jennifer finished the details of the story: The bouncer, embarrassed to no end, quit his job and had his final check mailed to him. One of the other bouncers, a good friend of JT's, said he would never show his face in that club again. She added that the club's owner deducted a cleaning fee from his final check. Even with the cleaning, she said the smell still lingered for a few days. But the part she was most relieved about was JT's choice of meals prior to coming to the club. According to the other bouncer, JT was actually thinking of filing a complaint against the sushi bar, believing that it was the cause of his problem. Foul play was never suspected and Jennifer was in the clear.

I made a mental note to stay on these girls' good sides— if I started working there, that is. But by that time, I was pretty much convinced. I only hoped I wouldn't chicken out in the morning.

# 4

# Starting Out

*J* woke up the next morning eager and excited. Of course, I was extremely nervous, too, but I decided to go for it anyway. Even so, I completely chickened out for two days following my little Q & A with the girls. It was actually three days later that I threw caution to the wind and drove to the club. Yes, I was still wrestling with a few issues. The nudity aspect was my biggest concern. Exactly how would I react when the time to bare all arrived? And how would I feel about being mostly naked on the job, day after day, week after week, month after month? The other issue that gave me pause was the very real possibility that someone I knew would eventually show up at the club and see me dancing in little more than my birthday suit. A friend, a classmate, an ex-boyfriend (I was attending college in my home state)—discovery by any of those individuals would be more than embarrassing, it would be mortifying.

But I had already convinced myself that this was something I *needed* to do. More important, I knew I would regret it immensely if I didn't go through with it. My only out was the fact that I hadn't been offered the job yet. Perhaps I would botch the audition completely or totally freeze up under pressure and get turned away like a carnivore at a vegetarian buffet.

I would find out soon enough.

When I finally arrived at the club—I stopped more than half a dozen times along the way, considering whether or not to turn around and forget it—it was almost six o'clock. The place wasn't very busy, but there were customers and the dancers were doing their thing. Originally, my plan was to have a drink and calm my nerves, but when I learned that Nikki and Bunny hadn't arrived yet, I figured I'd get the audition process over with before they showed up. This way, if I did blow it, I could get out of there and save myself the humiliation of having to retell my sob story.

So, without any alcohol in my system, I bravely soldiered ahead and asked for the manager, using Bunny and Nikki as references. Like the Lou Albano look-alike I previously encountered, club manager Dave was also short and fat, but he was completely clean-shaven—head, cheeks, and chin. Kojak without the lollipop—or the body or the looks or the charm. But based on his girth, I was certain he didn't pass up too many sweets. He wore an assortment of large gold rings, a beefy nugget-style gold bracelet, a gold watch that might have been larger than London's Big Ben, and a Mr. T starter kit around his neck. Many of his gold chains were adorned with various charms, the largest being an Italian horn made of jade. Seated at the bar, he was watching a baseball game on television when I introduced myself and explained that I was interested in dancing there.

First, he looked me up and down, as if he were a sculptor searching for imperfections on his newest creation. Then he looked me up and down again, this time lingering on various areas—areas I'd been taught my whole life to keep covered. Had he stared any longer, I might have suggested he take a photograph, but I held my tongue. I knew popping off to the boss would definitely not start my stripping career off on the right foot. After a bit, he took my hand, curling his ring-adorned sausage-like fingers around mine, and invited me to sit down for a bit to tell him about myself. Rebecca and Jennifer had prepared me for this—Dave wants you to feel like he's your buddy, they'd said—so I obliged him.

Without going into too much detail, I told him I was a student, simply looking to pick up some extra cash.

Dave turned to the bartender, busy mixing up a cocktail. "What do you think? Can we use another girl?"

"We can *always* use another girl," the bartender said with a lecherous smile. "I know I could."

Dave laughed, then turned back to me. "Did you bring anything to dance in? You have to audition before you can join my harem."

No shit I have to audition, I wanted to say. I may have been totally new to the strip biz, but I was savvy enough to know that a girl would still have to show her stuff before she was offered a job, although Rebecca told me that at this club, just like many of the others she had worked at, all you needed were tits and a heartbeat to get hired. Dave's harem comment made me want to skip the audition and look into working at another club, but I liked the idea of having two allies—Jennifer and Rebecca—to help me out if I had any problems or questions. So I just held up my bag and nodded.

Dave pointed to the dressing room. "Good. Go get changed. Come back when you're ready and we'll see what you can do."

As I walked back to the dressing room, the butterflies in my stomach that I had contended with all night, all morning, and the entire drive to the club returned—with about a million of their friends. My lips got dry, my throat parched, and I felt as if I was going to break out in hives any second. Normally, I'm not a nervous person, but the thought of auditioning for the manager really got to me. It would be bad enough dancing topless for paying customers, but I figured that with other girls around me, all doing the exact same thing, I wouldn't feel as alone and exposed and vulnerable. Now, I'd be doing it solo, under Dave's piercing stare, and I was damn sure he'd be looking at me like a picky Olympic figure-skating judge (hopefully, not a French judge!), scouring my body and technique for flaws and imperfections, or envisioning doing things to me that were just too vile to think about.

Then again, there was the possibility that he had seen so many strippers audition over the years that this screening process was exactly as Rebecca had said it would be: just a minor formality to make sure that I had some semblance of rhythm and that I didn't just stand there swaying back and forth like a piece of straw in the breeze.

But Dave struck me as a real control freak, not to mention a pervert, and the more I thought about him and the audition, the more nervous I became.

Breathe, Lacey, breathe, I told myself as I put on my dancewear. I'd brought three different outfits to pick from, a combination of thong bikini bottoms and sexy lingerie I'd owned for a year. After some pondering, I wound up going with black bottoms, a black lace wrap, and a clingy black top with an invisible zipper. For shoes, I climbed into the tallest sleaziest stilettos in my collection. They added four inches of height, slimmed my legs—which were freshly shaved and looked pretty good to begin with—and doubled as lethal weapons just in case Dave, or anyone else, got out of control. Like I said, I had no idea what to expect.

Glancing in the mirror before I went back out into the club, I honestly thought I *looked* great, albeit a little slutty—

although I figured that would be good for the audition. How I *felt*, on the other hand, was a totally different matter. If I'd had anything in my stomach other than the ginger ale I drank while driving to the club, I'm dead certain I would have deposited it into the toilet—or on the dressing room floor.

I remained in the dressing room for approximately 15 more minutes after getting changed, my subconscious mind actively trying to convince the fully alert side of my brain to pack up my stuff, run back to my car, and get the fuck out of there. Eventually, the oft-hidden but ever-present daredevil side of me won out and I headed out to confront my demons—figuratively and, considering the audience, literally.

When I got back to the bar, Dave was ready—along with the bartender, one of the bouncers (a massive farm-boy type wearing overalls and a tank-top), and a few other customers that I'm certain Dave *recruited* for the purpose of my audition.

"Are you ready?" Dave asked upon my return. "You look a little queasy."

"No, I'm fine," I lied. "Ready whenever you are."

"Okay. How's your balance?" he asked.

"Fine," I replied, curious as to where he was going with that question. "Why?"

"Well, I normally like to try girls out on stage, just to see how they handle it. But since it's being used, I thought you could use the bar."

A wave of panic swept over me. The stage, although not a huge platform by any means, was one hell of a lot wider than the bar. While I never had any problems with my balance before, I'd never done any gymnastics either, and I certainly wasn't a cat. Still, I was determined to gut it out and press on, no matter what Dave threw at me.

Trying to seize control of the situation, I reached out to the boy-faced bouncer. "Give a lady a hand," I said.

"Sure," the hulking Hee-Haw said. He grabbed me under my arms, lifted me with ease, and plopped me down on the bar, onto my butt.

Not quite what I had in mind, but it got the job done. The moment he stepped back, I swung my legs across, but the counter must have been recently wiped down or polished because I over-rotated, spinning until my legs were now hanging over the bar onto the bartender's side, causing Dave and the others to break into laughter. Before I could correct myself, the bartender came to my rescue. He gave my feet a gentle push, as if I were on a merry-go-round, and spun me back around. This time, I stopped myself in the proper position and extended my legs so that I was lying on my side across the bar. The laughter from the onlookers quickly transformed into claps and whistles. Admittedly, I was impressed with my quick recovery. Of course, my heart was still beating like a snare drum being worked by a kid with A.D.D.

After taking a moment to silently wish myself luck and encouragement, I brought my legs in and popped to my feet. Had I known I was to be dancing atop the bar, I would have chosen different shoes, but I wasn't about to let my towering (and slightly unsteady) heels stop me now. This was my big moment, the chance to look my unwanted self-doubting demons squarely in the eyes. Unfortunately, I accidentally kicked an ashtray and sent it flying. The bartender made an effort to grab it, but a gifted wide receiver he wasn't; the glass butt-holder hit the ground and shattered. *Shit!* Here I was, 30 seconds into a potential ego-saving cash-producing new job and I already *owed* money.

But I went on with the audition, forgetting about all the onlookers, just as I believed the redheaded girl did when she performed her lap-dance for me. Cheryl Lynn's "Got To Be Real" was playing, a song I really liked, and I got into the beat easily.

I started off moving slowly, I mean molasses S-L-O-W-L-Y, trying to work my way into the core of the beat. I wasn't sure exactly how I should be moving, but I thought that emulating sex—swiveling my hips, gyrating my torso, grinding the air, etc.—would be a pretty decent way to go. Granted, some of the moves were hard to mimic while standing, but for the most part I think I did okay.

Soon, I forgot I was perched atop a bar (well, sort of) and thought only of the music's rhythm, freeing my body to move in synch with the beat. I peeled my bottom wrap off seductively and hardly heard the whistles and catcalls that followed. Ditto for my top; I was now just a skimpy T-back away from full nudity, showing off to total strangers hidden treasures that very few men had seen up until then, and the best part about it was that I was becoming more at ease with the situation. Or maybe I was an exhibitionist at heart. Or I was in what athletes often refer to as *the zone*. Or I was so goddamn petrified that nothing mattered. Whatever the case, inside, I was celebrating. I truly felt liberated. Everything was going perfectly.

And then I made my final mistake.

Running horizontally above my head, perfectly visible from my bar-top vantage point, was a long pipe. The pipe ran the length of the bar and disappeared into the walls. Now, had I been on stage I would have been able to swing from the pole like a proper stripper would. (While I had never done that before, how hard could it possibly be?) But since I was dancing on the bar and this was the only "pole" available to me, easily within my reach, I figured I'd improvise and really impress Dave and the others.

In one smooth motion, I reached up with both hands, grabbed onto the pipe, lifted my legs into the air, and spread them into a wide V, really playing to the crowd. It was the sleaziest thing I had ever done—never in a million years could I have imagined doing such a thing—but I was now in *stripper mode* and determined to get the job. The last thing I wanted was to get turned down—or worse, have to repeat the audition—because I was too prude. With my legs still spread, I locked my eyes on Dave and gave him my most seductive smile, expecting to see him melt or drool.

Instead, his eyes bulged out of his head as if he were a cartoon character and he exploded to his feet, screaming at me, "Get the fuck off the water pipe!"

I almost let go exactly as I was, which would have resulted in a nasty fall and a sure trip to the emergency room. But I had enough sense to lower my feet to the bar and release the pipe as he had instructed.

"That's it," he said, motioning me to get down. "Audition's over."

While Dave just stood there with his hands on his hips, obviously still incensed, the bouncer helped me down from the bar. I felt terribly vulnerable standing there in front of Dave and the others—most of whom were laughing their asses off—wearing next to nothing, but for some reason I didn't rush to put my clothes back on. Perhaps that would have made me feel more naked than I already was.

Dave called me, among other things, Calamity Jane, said I was an accident waiting to happen, and it was a damn good thing I didn't pull the pipe off the ceiling or else my first week's wages would be going into a plumber's pocket instead of mine. I sifted through what he said, replaying his words until it dawned on me, and I brightened.

"Wait a minute," I said in disbelief. "I got the job?"

"Yeah, you got the job," he said, as if it should have been an assumed fact. "Just try not to destroy my club."

"Sorry about the ashtray," I said, trying to contain my excitement. After all, a real pro wouldn't be overcome with joy after getting a job at a run-of-the-mill strip club. But I was thrilled to death. For me, it was a major achievement.

"Don't worry about it," Dave said, giving me the first

indication he was human. "Maybe dancing on the bar wasn't such a good idea." He looked at his watch. "Can you work tonight? It should get busy pretty soon and I could use an extra girl."

Already there and in the flow, I was ready to rock. "Absolutely," I said with gusto.

"Good. Go see Gary," he said, pointing to the DJ booth. "He'll put you in the stage rotation. At the end of the night, come see me about the tip-out. I'll give you a break since it's your first night."

"Thank you, Dave," I replied sincerely, even though I didn't know what the hell a tip-out was. But I figured if he was giving me a break on anything, I might as well be appreciative about it.

With the audition out of the way, the rest of the night was a cakewalk. I had a bit of a hard time using the stage pole the first few times—the girls make it look much easier than it is—but eventually I got the hang of it. I didn't try anything really elaborate, although at the end of one routine I slid down face-first and bumped my head on the floor. Luckily, it was dark and no one seemed to notice. The next time I tried it, I managed to stop myself with my legs at the last moment.

I didn't do any VIP Room dances that night, which is probably just as well. I think I would have been too nervous to do a good job, plus neither Jennifer nor Rebecca—or any of the other girls, for that matter—told me what they charged for lap-dances in the VIP Room. No one told me about a lot of things. But looking back, discovering how things worked, on my own, at my own pace, was definitely the right way to go. If for no other reason, it made me feel as if I truly deserved to be there.

By the end of the night, I had a much greater respect for strippers. Prior to my indoctrination into the world of topless dancing, I'd never given any thought to dancers and how hard they worked for their money. Like so many others, I simply bestowed on them a cheesy label, never stopping to consider that what they do—and what I did—isn't easy. It's extremely taxing on the body; it's mentally draining, as well. That's not saying you need to be a *Solid Gold* dancer or have the body of a *Playboy* centerfold to make a buck in the topless biz—you don't. But you do need a good supply of moxie and the tolerance to deal with an assortment of people—from multimillionaire perfect gentlemen to the absolute pigs of humanity—on a daily basis. Topless dancing is customer service to the extreme.

My first night in the biz ended just after one in the morning. I was wiped out physically and my knees were aching big-time—*you* try dancing in high-heels for a few hours and see how you feel! However, I was really proud of myself for going through with it; I felt like I'd gotten an 'A' on a term paper that I'd worked on for months.

After my last dance, I met with club manager Dave, as instructed, where I learned about the tip-out procedure. Most strip clubs have a similar protocol: A dancer gives a percentage of her nightly haul to be divvied up by the DJ, bartender, doormen, and the house-mom (if the club employs one). Fortunately, this club didn't, which meant more money for me. After parting with ten percent of my earnings, I still walked away with close to $300. Not a stellar amount to be sure, but for my first night, for only six hours of work, I was extremely pleased. Actually, for my first night as a full-fledged stripper, the money was the icing on the cake.

Jennifer and Rebecca wanted to go out and celebrate, but more than anything I just wanted to go home and take a bath. My adrenaline rush had subsided by then and, more than feeling tired, I felt dirty. Grungy, actually. Like how those "Survivors" probably feel at the end of their stint on the island. That bath was one of the best in my life.

The next day, I decided to spend my hard-earned cash on a few little extravagances, things I really didn't need but truly wanted—new shoes, a new purse, a cool hat or two. The way I shopped, $300 would go a long long way. Now, I'm no cheapskate, no frugal Freeda, but I could never understand how someone could go out and spend a thousand dollars and come back with only one outfit. Maybe that was fine for the Rodeo Drive set, but I could turn a $100 bill into an entire wardrobe—a damn fine one, too.

I worked four days straight that first week, earning a total of $1,900, $700 of which came in one night, the bulk of it from one guy. He was my first VIP Room customer and I quickly learned that the VIP Room was where the real action was and where most strippers wanted to spend the majority of their time.

Strangely, some girls actually preferred table- and lap-dances in the main club over dances in the VIP Room. Not this chick! Why anyone would want to work twice as hard for half the money when they could get a customer (or customers) into the back room and really do some damage to their wallets was beyond me.

By the end of that first week, the butterfiles had all flown off and the nudity didn't make a dent in my consciousness. I began to look at stripping as a challenge. Exactly how much money could I get (fleece) from each and every guy who asked me to dance for him? More than a job or a challenge, it was a game—cat and mouse, in a way—and I realized that inside the strip clubs, the women were clearly the cats. We were the *hunters*.

But the most important realization from that first week was my proclivity for the profession. Granted, I had a lot to learn and I was certain to make numerous mistakes along the way, but I knew I was good at it. *Real* good. And I had the potential to be great. And the thing of it was, it had nothing to do with my looks. It was all about personality and panache. The best salespeople in the world sell themselves first and their products second. In the exotic entertainment industry, the topless dancer herself *is* the product. The way I saw it, I was going to be one of the hottest products on the market, pulling the plug on a couple decades worth of low confidence and feelings of worthlessness in the process.

# 5

# Sink or Swim

*I*'ve always been a fast learner. No matter how hard the subject or the task, I caught on quickly. Working as a topless dancer was no exception.

But in the world of exotic entertainment, learning the ropes expeditiously isn't just beneficial—it's a necessity. That is, if earning top dollar is your number-one priority. In my case, breaking out of my self-constructed mental prison was the main concern. However, getting the job went a long way toward that end and just showing up to work would take me the rest of the way. Beyond that, I was committed to being as financially productive as possible each and every second I spent in the club. Stripping was a job, one that required a tremendous amount of effort, and I was determined to treat it as such. Nothing less than max input was on my agenda.

The topless business is like a vast ocean, and each dancer in it has three choices. She can sink, which ultimately means her time would be better spent working at Burger King.

She can tread water, which amounts to steady money that pays the bills and little more. Or she can swim, thus maximizing the earning potential. Well, not only did I want to swim, I wanted to do a brisk breaststroke across the sea, get to the other side, and run on the beach with my hair blowing in the wind!

For the first few weeks I kept my eyes and ears open, taking in everything that happened around me, processing it like a computer would raw data. I listened to the other dancers—what they had to say about each other and the job, in general. And I listened to the customers, who were the final authority on how much I took home on a nightly basis. It didn't take me long to realize I could do different things to better my chances of financial success—lots of little tricks that meant the difference between an okay night ($300) and a great night ($1,000). By the same token, I discovered there were also practices to avoid—actions that could potentially turn off a customer and lock out my access to his billfold. Of all my discoveries—and there were many—the biggest breakthrough occurred, fortunately, early on. It was simply this: to spend as much of my time as possible dancing for customers in the VIP Room.

It was obvious from the get-go that the stage was geared for the masses—there was plenty to see and it was plenty cheap. If a dancer made $50 during her turn on stage, she was really kicking ass. To the untrained eye, a near-endless flow of singles (and occasionally fives) may seem like a treasure trove, but compared to what could be made doing table dances or lap dances—or even better yet, VIP Room dances—it was chicken feed.

Lap and table dances are the next rungs up the loot ladder from the stage. Often, it was the stint on stage that got you noticed and selected—but not always. Many times I was simply walking by when I was asked for a lap dance. Mostly though, I took the proactive approach. I homed in on the guys I believed had the gangster rolls in their front pockets and did all I could to relieve them of every cent they had with them—not to mention whatever they could get from their ATM and/or credit cards. You have to understand, my intent wasn't malicious, and I hate to come across sounding like a shark circling a wounded diver. It's just the nature of the business. Always was and always will be. The funny thing is, most of the men who go to strip clubs know the ins and outs of the biz as well as the dancers. They, too, are playing the game—trying to get as much as they can for as little as possible. But the strippers will *always* have the upper hand. That's not to say that no dancers get taken advantage of. Like any profession's practitioners, there are those who are simply not cut out for the work and the mindset it requires. Devoid of club smarts, they might accept $50, or less, to do something another dancer wouldn't even consider for under $200. I'm just generalizing, but a stripper needs to understand her environment, and know that *she* makes the rules. Failing that, she'd be much better off working in a traditional 9-to-5 gig with a punch card and a lunch break and a list of guaranteed benefits.

Anyway, in regard to lap and table dances, they're merely financial appetizers. Dancers can make decent money performing them, but the main course is the VIP Room, where per-dance prices usually double or triple (or more, depending on the club). Tips also skyrocket in the VIP Rooms. The more intimate contact has a tendency to open a man's wallet. However, you still have to get the customer *to* the VIP Room—and know how to keep him there once you do—but that's all part of the game. A game I intended to play to the bone.

Of course, every customer who visits a strip club is different—different background, different wants, different needs, etc.—but I learned a host of techniques that could be applied to nearly every man (and occasional woman) who came in.

The first was direct eye contact. Customers love to be singled out, even if it's only for a second. Pinning a guy in your stare is the equivalent of hooking a fish. All that needs to be done after that is land him. For instance, if I was on stage, while playing to the crowd I would also try to single out the one guy in the place I thought was the treasure chest of the moment. In the beginning of my topless tenure, this was easier said than done. I learned the hard way that just because a guy is dressed to the nines doesn't mean he's a real player. From a distance, in the shadowy atmosphere of a strip club, an off-the-rack Brooks Brothers suit looks identical to a custom Armani. And just because a guy is tossing singles to stage dancers like they were water, it's wrong to assume he'll be a big spender in the VIP Room. It might just be because he's drunk, as I discovered on more than one occasion.

But as I became more experienced, the selection process became more natural. Women's intuition had a lot to do with it, that little voice inside my head that guided me along. So did simple observation: How a man handles himself says a truckload about his financial status. At least, it did more often than it didn't. But mostly it was trial and error. A poor choice usually netted a scathingly low haul, in most cases the fee for the private dance—*one* private dance—and nothing more. Then it would be back to the drawing board, looking for the next guy. In essence, a wasted opportunity. But everyone has to learn the hard way, which is better than not learning at all.

Anyway, direct eye contact was especially important during the lap dances themselves, especially in the VIP Room. Even though I was just going through the motions, with no more real feeling for a guy than if he were simply a barrel of cash that I was systematically trying to empty, to him it was a fantasy, a pleasurable adventure that could last as long as he wanted it to (or, perhaps more appropriately, as long as his money supply lasted). I needed to make him feel as if I truly wanted to be there, with him, although it was quite possible I was thinking about redecorating my apartment or adding to my wardrobe the entire time. A customer had to know, without question, that I was his—no questions, end of story—and pinning him in my stare, eyes conveying a sense of companionship and sensuality, and possibility, was the first step.

Another important aspect of strip club success is the ability to role-play. Mind you, I'm not talking about dressing up as a cop or a nurse or a Girl Scout—although costumes do work wonders. No, I'm talking about determining exactly what type of woman a customer wants you to be, then delivering on that character. For example, there were guys who I knew, beyond a shadow of a doubt, would have been turned off (pronounced *afraid*) of intellectual women. Any girl who could converse using words with more than two syllables would have sent them running. When I encountered guys like that, I automatically lowered my IQ by about 50 points. I could play the ditzy airhead with the best of them and some guys just ate it up. They wanted to feel superior, that they knew the ways of the world and the vagaries of life and I was merely a cog in the wheel, content to put on my make-up and high heels and look pretty for them. Guys like that were cake to manipulate. Others were looking for someone to talk at, to listen to their bragging or their sob stories or their views on the world, offering nothing more than an occasional nod or a "wow," "impressive," or "I'm sorry." Some actually wanted a dancer to interact with them, discussing anything from current events to the weather, from mutual funds to the no-hitter some guy with a last name I couldn't pronounce tossed the other night.

Role-playing required you to be a good listener, waiting for the tip-off that indicated exactly what kind of character the customer preferred. And that meant you had to be flexible and fast on your feet, able to drop into character the moment you figured it out. As you might expect, at times I guessed wrong. For example, one time I pegged this guy as a slow-starter looking for an aggressive woman to get his juices, and his cash, flowing. But when I came on like gangbusters, he clamped shut tighter than a frightened oyster. As it turned out, I'd made a costly mistake; a little while later, he made another dancer's night, shelling out more than $500.

On those occasions, I either dug my way out of the small hole I'd made for myself by playing it off in a goofy manner—blamed it on the booze, his pheromone-activating cologne, or some other obscure but plausible reason—or I simply accepted the fact that I was probably going to get a shitty tip, no tip, or lose the customer to another dancer. Once again, it was all just a part of the game and I learned not to take it personally.

That leads me to another crucial aspect of working in a topless joint: attitude. You can be butt-ugly, out of shape, and dumber than a pair of sweat-socks with the dancing ability of a one-legged drunk and *still* make a fair amount of money if you have a good attitude. Trust me, I've seen it done time and time again. But throw a shitty attitude into the mix and I promise you the only thing you'll go home with is sore feet.

Attitude is, in my opinion, the main reason why some dancers excel and many others don't. Too many girls come into work with a piss-poor attitude, complaining about this, that, or the other thing, make next to nothing, and leave even more pissed off than when they arrived.

One night, at a club where I was working in California, an established feature entertainer (a former centerfold in one of the major adult skin magazines and a real up-and-cummer—pun intended—in the XXX biz) came in to perform. Apparently, she'd gotten into a fight with her boyfriend/manager in the limousine on the way to the club.

The second she walked into the dressing room I could tell she was in a sour mood. Immediately, she began to complain. The dressing room was too cold, the stage was too short, the pole was too wide, the lighting was too bright, the customers looked too poor—you name it, she had a problem with it. But I guess she figured her goddess-like body and looks would compensate for her suck-monkey demeanor. Wrong! I wasn't surprised at all when she cut her routine short and left in a huff. I think the flower girl made more than she did that night.

While I'm by no means professing to be Miss Congeniality 24/7/365, I decided early on that when I went into the club to work, anything that had happened outside the club *stayed* outside the club. If I found myself unable to put on a smile and act like I truly wanted to be there, I simply wouldn't go in. I almost always rose to the task, but those times when I just knew the night would be a total bust, I avoided the club like the plague. Men are there to see tits and ass, yes, but they're certainly not going to shell out major coin to girls dancing for them with permanent scowls, I don't care how gorgeous they are.

At one club, there was a black girl named Darci who, had she wanted to, probably could have been a Victoria's Secret catalog model or a *Sports Illustrated* swimsuit-issue model. Tall, femininely muscular, and absolutely beautiful, she was easily one of the most attractive women I had ever seen. But Darci had a major attitude problem. From the in-club rumor mill (every strip club has one), I heard that much of it stemmed from a failing marriage, along with a deep appreciation for vodka. At the beginning of the night she would be peaches 'n cream to all who came into contact with her, dancers and customers alike. But midway through the shift, Darci transformed into King Kong in a thong and everyone within a mile was well-advised to steer clear of her. I figured she was not long for the business—at least at that club—and the circumstances of her final night didn't surprise me in the least.

Apparently, a VIP Room customer was less than pleased with Darci's performance and tipped her a dollar, in quarters, to make a point. By that time, Darci's chip was practically crushing her shoulder and she decided to make a point of her own. First, she spit in the customer's face—a nasty green globule she seemed to conjure up from her soul. Had she ended it there, perhaps she would have only been suspended from the club for a week or so, if at all. But the phlegmy facial wasn't enough and she followed it up with a straight right to the guy's chops, chipping one of his teeth with her ring in the process. After some serious negotiating, financial reparations, and major freebies, the customer agreed not to file charges or sue. Darci, of course, received her walking papers. On the way out, she spit on the floor, the manager, and the bouncer, too. I don't expect you'll find her working in Customer Service any time soon!

While the attitude of the dancer is a key element of her success, the attitude of the customer is equally important—though often overlooked. Dancers have to be able to determine when a customer is truly interested and willing to spend a lot of money on her, as opposed to when he's simply biding his time, shining her on, trying to get more for less. This determination is something a dancer needs to make immediately, for it will set the financial tone of the evening, and her career. If a dancer believes she can make more money via volume—meaning many one- and two-song dances for numerous customers—more power to her. But in my opinion, that's working way too hard for way too little of a reward. The best way for a dancer to hit the jackpot is to latch on to a customer (or customers), develop a (working) relationship of sorts, and take him for all he's worth. Again, there's nothing vindictive about that statement, and I certainly don't mean to sound rapacious, but that's how it works.

This is how it was done long before I broke into the biz and this is how it will be done for eons to come—assuming our nation doesn't become a complete Big Brother society and legislation shuts down the strip club industry.

Many guys go to strip clubs planning to spend more on booze than on the girls. These are the customers you want to identify and steer clear of. Don't waste time chatting it up with a guy like that—you're probably only going to get one or two dances out of him—when other men out there are ready and willing to pay for four, five, or six dances. Spotting one of these liquor-loving tightwads isn't always easy. Befriend a cocktail waitress or two and ask them to keep track of any power-drinking customers. Ditto for the bartenders. The courtesy $5 or $10 you shell out for the info might save you from wasting your time—and losing serious money—in the long run.

In the Vegas clubs, the girls can drink for free, but in many other cities the dancers are charged for their cocktails. In these clubs, if a customer is initially hesitant about paying for a lap dance, at least get him to buy a couple of drinks— one for you and one for him. Alcohol has a tendency to loosen up customers, along with the ties to their wallets. I've had some of my best nights courtesy of guys who, at first, weren't at all interested in paying for a lap dance or journeying to the VIP Room, and it all started with a casual getting-to-know-you cocktail. However, some dancers take advantage of the drink freebies and get themselves too soused to work. I'd often see girls getting wasted with customers, which in some cases didn't hurt their earnings, as the guys were looking for companions for the night, not necessarily dancers. But on other occasions, when it came time to perform and the girls were unable to, they were dropped like yesterday's news in favor of dancers who had all their faculties. Waking up with empty pockets *and* a hangover is clearly not the way to make it big in the topless business.

I made a pact with myself when I first started dancing that when I went to work, I worked. Often, I'd see girls taking break after break, chatting it up in the dressing room with other girls, constantly talking on their cell phones, or simply hiding out in the bathroom with a cigarette and a glass of wine. It was usually those same girls who complained at the end of the night, week, or month that they didn't have enough to make their rent or car payment. To be successful as a stripper, you need to circulate. You absolutely have to put yourself in position to make money and that means getting around and getting seen. Four-figure nights with millionaire celebrity customers do occur, but they're few and far between. On most nights (and/or days), strippers have to grind it out, figuratively and literally, making $20 here, $40 there, and so on. It takes real effort and those who aren't committed to working—and working hard— are probably better served in a different profession.

Alcoholic beverages aside, there are other "tricks" a dancer can use to get guys in the mood and eager to spend. For instance, when I knew guys were watching, I might come up and give another dancer a smack on the ass, playful but firm, which almost always triggered a positive response from the surrounding males. Most men are entranced by girl-on-girl and two-girl/one-guy fantasies. Just the thought of becoming the meat in a girlie sandwich drives them through the roof and every stripper knows it. (Actually, I think all women are born with this knowledge—must be some kind of neonatal-instilled feminine characteristic.) Many of those gentle pats resulted in trips to the VIP Room, often with a favorable ratio of dancers to customers—and we all banked the bucks.

Another trick of the trade involved my stage performances. In most cases, this is when a dancer does the most and earns the least. Unfortunately, every dancer has to take her turn on stage (or stages, depending on the club's layout). To maximize my time, I often enlisted the help of a small prop to up the ante. For some reason, watching a woman rub some sort of object on or across her body is more appealing to most men than simply watching that woman caress herself with her hands. Don't ask me why. Maybe somebody should do a study on it. (Hell, they've spent our tax dollars on weirder things!) Besides, I'd sure as hell like to know the results.

My favorite prop was a loaded water pistol (even fake guns are great attention-getters). Not only could I rub it against my body but it was perfect for singling guys out of the crowd. All it took was a playful squirt and they were mine—my version of big-game hunting. Sometimes, I even filled it with liquor—usually vodka or rum—and topped a guy's drink off for free if he desired. The $10 or so it cost me to fill it up at the beginning of the night almost always came back ten- or twenty-fold. I got the idea from another stripper who used a toy slingshot to fire Hershey's Kisses at the guys she wanted to entertain after her turn on stage. Sure, the water pistol was a case of one-upsmanship but, hey, that's what it's all about.

Other dancers used props, too, and some of the items—and the manner in which they were used—were extremely creative. Others were freaky and sick. I've seen strippers use dildos (external use only on stage, but who knows what the hell they did behind closed doors), hula-hoops, martial-arts weapons like samurai swords and *nunchakus*, pieces of rope, chains, a straitjacket (she was a better escape artist than Houdini), a broom, chocolate chips and a mini-vacuum, playing cards (one dancer even played an erotic game of *War* with the customers closest to the stage), power tools of varying sizes, lotions and oils, and all types of food items including whipped cream, chocolate syrup, assorted puddings, and one extra-long zucchini.

One of the coolest routines I ever watched involved a

pair of custom nipple covers. They were made of some kind of synthetic material and the dancer wet them, stuck them to her breasts, coated them with a flammable liquid like lighter fluid, and set them on fire. Although they didn't burn for very long, it was long enough to get the guys *all* hot and bothered. Then, with her fingertips coated with cream or Vaseline, she pinched her nipples and snuffed out the flames. Definitely original.

Perhaps the most unusual routine I ever saw involved a large trained rat. Shelly, as limber a person as I've seen, contorted her body in all different ways, while the rat scurried from one limb to another, over her boobs, across her back, onto her head, down her butt, and never once did it touch the ground. It was really outrageous and guys went wild. Something about a woman and a rodent, I guess.

Another solid self-marketing ploy was the dirty joke. I always made sure I knew at least one really good joke involving sex, one that I could tell without fail. Many times, this was the perfect icebreaker that conveyed I was not only playful in a provocative way, but that I had a sense of humor, too. Fun girls made more money than bump-on-a-log girls no matter what they looked like.

Bouncers were also great allies in the quest to make big money. When I was comfortable at a club, I took the doormen aside, separately, and gave them a few bucks, letting them know there was more where that came from if they recommended my lap-dance services to potential big-shot customers. Any guys arriving in limos or mega-dollar sports cars, I wanted them to ask for me by name. In these situations, $10 or $20 every now and then went a long way.

Most clubs in the country have what is referred to as a "Touch and Go" policy: If a customer touches a dancer, it's time for him to go. However, dancers routinely initiate contact with the customers and no one would say boo about it. It's a double standard for sure, but it's a mandate that exists for the strippers' protection. The no-touch policy also applies to the VIP Room, but in those private confines each dancer decides exactly what she's going to allow—and for how much she'll allow it.

One of my best tricks for hooking a big fish was the 10-second massage. If I was looking for a VIP Room prospect, I would come up behind a guy and give him a tantalizing neck or shoulder rub for about 10 seconds, then quickly move on to another guy, usually someone he was seated with or near. The idea was to spawn a bidding war of sorts, to get one of them to jump first at the chance to lock up my services. Sometimes, guys didn't really even want the dance, but it came down to a pissing contest, some kind of machismo thing, which no red-blooded American male wants to lose, especially in the company of women and his peers.

All the successful dancers rely on a battery of tricks and gimmicks to boost their earnings. Don't get me wrong, straight-out sex appeal is a powerful weapon in the stripping business and many girls use their bodies and looks and nothing more to earn a decent living. But from my experience, the girls who use their brains first and foremost go home each night with the boo-coo bucks. Ask any of the older dancers who still bring home the bacon and I'm sure they'll agree. Beauty only lasts so long, especially with the rigors of the topless profession. Intelligence, on the other hand, is there for the duration. So if you've got the smarts, you might as well put them to good use.

Unfortunately, a host of strippers out there have the brainpower of daffodils. This is not a slight to the women of the profession by any means: Just as many women working in the myriad of other jobs are severely lacking in the intelligence department. For these dancers, their bodies are not just their best props—they're their *only* props.

In most cases, when the word "stripper" is first uttered, images of a sculpted, toned, big-breasted woman with the sexuality of a porn star are what come to mind. In many of the hotter strip clubs, it's not far from the truth. However, you needn't look like Kristy Swanson or Pamela Anderson to break the bank while working as a topless dancer. Sure, it doesn't hurt, and women blessed with smoking looks and killer bodies obviously have an advantage in a skin palace, but only when it comes to customers looking for exactly that kind of woman.

Contrary to popular belief, not all men desire the centerfold-quality sexpot: long flowing hair, large firm breasts with diamond-hard nipples, no waist, and legs that go on until Tuesday … That's the Hollywood version of the perfect stripper. In the real world I've seen nights where women with more rolls than a Jewish bakery made twice or three times as much as the sexiest girls in the place. Tastes vary—in food, cars, clothes, lifestyles, and especially in what a customer is looking for in a stripper. While certain clubs are known for the "quality" of their dancers—Scores in Manhattan is a prime example, where rumor has it you need to be a 9½, minimum, on the 1 to 10 scale to get a job—other clubs employ a more diverse coterie of dancers, an all-shapes-and-sizes smorgasbord of tits and ass.

It's for those reasons that I laugh when I see a program like Jerry Springer or Jenny Jones, when the topic is: "You're Too Nasty To Be A Stripper" or something to that effect. On those programs, the scene is usually a bunch of obese women in thongs shaking like jello molds in an earthquake while the audience is booing and hissing. If a woman (or a man, for that matter) has it in mind that she (or he) can make some coin by dropping trou and shaking ass, regardless of how big or unsightly it may be, I say more power to her. There's no strip club rule I'm aware of that states: Only goddesses need apply. During my years as a topless dancer, I met countless women you'll never see on any looks-driven reality dating shows, all of whom made upwards of $50,000 a year courtesy of their lack of inhibition. As a society, we tend to chastise people we're uncomfortable with when we should be applauding them for having the courage to simply be themselves. In the case of a so-called "unsightly stripper," there's no gun to your head. All you have to do is look away.

On the other hand, for the women who are in fantastic shape or strive for physical perfection, they have their work cut out for them. Eating right, working out, getting the proper amount of rest, they're all part of the regimen. Working in the topless dancing industry, with its late hours, physical demands, and constant exposure to booze and cigarettes (and for some, drugs), can play havoc with a desire to stay fit. This is a subject on which I can definitely speak from experience. Having always been concerned about my body and appearance (especially when I was stripping), I went on dieting binges all the time, thinking I needed to drop weight to look my best. Other times, I finished work and, despite my exhaustion, donned a sweatsuit and went on some marathon run, trying to shed a few extra pounds, even if I was already at an optimum weight for my frame. Other girls spend hours in the gym, pushing their bodies to the limits, then starve themselves of some much-needed nourishment. It wasn't uncommon to see a dancer pass out in the dressing room after a few hours of work.

Many girls turn to laxatives and appetite suppressants and/or controlled substances (like coke or speed) to keep their weight in check, even if they never had a problem with it prior to becoming a stripper. They subscribe to the "better bodies through science" mindset, even though they're doing considerably more harm than good. Although bulimia is a nasty word in the strip club dressing room, one that's often whispered, but not spoken aloud, I can't begin to tell you how many times I heard girls gagging and vomiting in the bathroom stalls after they'd eaten.

Just like television and the movies, stripping is an image-obsessed profession. For some dancers, same as the entertainers on the small and big screens, perfection is an attainable condition. And whatever can't be achieved solo can be bestowed upon them with the help of a qualified physician.

For instance, a big night of tips in the VIP Room might translate into bigger breasts (via implants) the following week. The purchase of a few new outfits could be postponed in favor of collagen injections in the lips. Or a new nose and some liposuction can be financed instead of a new car. I knew girls who got into stripping to eliminate their debt, only to find themselves pouring every cent they earn into their bodies. One dancer, a beautiful girl with a body to match, went through four different breast augmentations, and four different cup sizes, in the span of two years. When last we spoke, I think she was a double-F and considering going larger. That's taking "hooked on phonics" to a whole new level! By comparison, my self-esteem issues were minor.

In case you're wondering, I'm all in favor of cosmetic surgery. I myself had my breasts enlarged and am delighted with the results. Although it was something I never considered doing while I was dancing, or in the years preceding, there came a point in time when I believed it would balance out my figure and enhance my overall physical appearance. So, when the timing—and my finances—were right, I went ahead and did it. It's all a matter of personal choice, but I bring it up because, in the exotic entertainment industry, it's not a mandatory requirement. Being beautiful means many things to many different people. For some, it's the kind of woman you'd find modeling a skimpy bikini in *Sports Illustrated*'s swimsuit issue; for others, it's the kind of woman making her third trip through the buffet line. That's what's so great about the topless profession: It takes all types. And anyone, with the right attitude, can be successful.

# 6

# Regulars

*E*very now and then some big-shot celebrity or super-wealthy businessman visits a strip club and throws cash around like it's Monopoly money. You hear about it happening all the time—Scores in New York City and the now defunct Gold Club in Atlanta, two clubs I never worked at—were always in the news, almost always because someone looking for a few extra bucks squealed to the tabloids. Just ask Charlie Sheen or Patrick Ewing. They were on the receiving end of the gossip stick on more than one occasion. Personally, I think it's a shame. I believe anyone who visits a strip club, whether it's a prudish bikini bar or a full-bore nudie joint, deserves his anonymity. Of course, managers and owners don't seem to mind. Any PR is good PR, or so the saying goes, and attention in the news almost always results in more customers. But having said that, depending on high rollers and big spenders for your income is not a wise course of action. The real key to making good money consistently is by developing a solid stable of regulars.

Chances are, if you treat a customer well and show him a good time, he'll come back. Again and again and again. Repeat business is a major aspect of the topless industry and the dancers absolutely depend on it.

One of the smartest things I ever did was set up a voice-mail service, which I used strictly for my regular customers. I would never even think of giving out my home phone number—not with all the crazy shit that goes on this world, especially in the sex industry—but there was no harm in providing them with my phone-service number. Coupled with the fact that I used an alias when I danced, I felt relatively safe. If a real nutcase wanted to get to me, no fake phone number or pseudonym would stop him anyway.

The idea was to stay in touch with my regulars and keep them coming in on a steady basis. After their initial call to my phone-service, I'd call them back every so often at the numbers they provided, hoping like hell I got an answering machine and not the actual person. It was much easier to leave seductive messages, dropping hints of possibility (if they were *good* to me), rather than talk to them directly. On those occasions when one of my regulars picked up the phone, I kept the conversation short and sweet, telling him I was late for a hair appointment or an exercise class or a waxing—whatever it took to end the call quickly but politely. I also made sure never to promise anything. I was asked out on numerous dates—for drinks, dinner, and even trips (from overnights to multi-week vacations)—but I never accepted. "I'd love to but I just can't right now" was a standard response that I (and many of the other strippers) relied upon. Bob and weave, duck and cover … You had to be like a prizefighter, a *successful* prizefighter, to refuse the offer cordially, while keeping the relationship open.

Often, I tried to set appointments, staggering guys who paid me well, so good money for the night's work was pretty much guaranteed. For example, I'd call one guy and tell him to come to the club on Friday at eight o'clock, and that I was only going to be working for a few hours. He'd be there like clockwork at 8, ready to go. I'd spend time with him for two hours or so—dancing, talking, whatever he wanted—then I'd walk him to the door, encouraging him to go home and get a good night's sleep or make love to his wife or fly to the moon. Whatever! Basically, I just wanted him out of there. The reason: I had another appointment with another regular, anywhere from 15 to 30 minutes after the previous one. Not that there was a problem having two regulars (or more) see each other or know about the other—we were just entertaining these guys, after all, not dating them—but it always helped to convey a sense of loyalty, especially if you wanted them to tip—and keep on tipping—you big. Not only that, but the less time a regular spent in the club when he wasn't with you, the more money he would have to lavish on you. After all, you were the one he came to see in the first place.

I remember one time when I was with one of my regulars, a guy from whom I usually made between $400 and $500 a night. On this occasion, a well-known porn star was performing in the club as a featured entertainer and she was auctioning off some prop from her most recent film—I think it was a piece of lingerie she wore in a really wild sex scene. Anyway, the bidding was up to $300 and climbing and my guy was leading the pack, throwing up his hand whenever someone outbid him. I was a bit peeved and tried to gently discourage him, offering to give him one of my sexy outfits for *free*. I knew that if he bought the item, he'd have nothing left. Sure enough, despite my efforts to convince him otherwise, he won the lingerie—spending something like $450 in the process—and only had $50 left for me. You can't win 'em all.

After about two years in the biz, I got smart and tried to make deals with one or two other dancers I thought I could trust. We agreed to take care of each other's regulars on the nights that they came in and we didn't. So if I was off one night and one of my top customers showed up, Candy made it a point to treat him right—assuming one of her regulars wasn't there—then gave me a percentage of the money she made. On her nights off, I did the same for her. Of course, this system wasn't foolproof—dancers could easily lie about their take and customers weren't about to fess up about what they spent on another dancer. I certainly wasn't about to ask them. But at least it was an attempt to profit from relationships that had already been cultivated. The key was finding other dancers you could trust—a tall order in the topless biz when money entered into the equation. During my seven-year stripping stint, I made this arrangement with only five girls. And of those five, I was pretty sure two of them were skimming from our original deal. It wasn't something I could prove—can you imagine seeing *that* case on "The People's Court"?—but my gut instincts were usually spot-on and I just had that feeling that I was being gypped. Needless to say, I terminated our agreement.

I worked at approximately 15 different clubs over the years. Often, I'd zip off to another city (in many cases, in an entirely different state) to dance for the weekend, just to keep things interesting and keep my mind fresh. Finding the happening clubs in other cities was a piece of cake; the g-string grapevine is long and widespread. Usually, at least one stripper has the full scoop on good clubs in neighboring cities and states, and is willing to share the information.

I found I grew bored easily when I spent too much time in the same environment and the variety helped me to enjoy the work. Sure, it was the same work, just different scenery, but the challenge of new fish to land added to the game. Sometimes I'd go with another dancer or two—to share the expenses or just for the old safety-in-numbers ploy—but more often I'd go by myself. At one point, I had a Rolodex filled with regulars and a full calendar of appointments—30 days solid—in three different states. I took a three-week much-needed vacation after that month. And that's another one of the benefits … Once a stripper has demonstrated to a club owner or manager that she'll bank the bucks whenever she works, 99 times out of 100 there'll be a spot for her in the rotation when she returns from a spur-of-the-moment vacation, regardless of how long she's gone.

There's a downside to dealing with regulars, however. Eventually, that extremely profitable relationship you worked so hard to build comes to an end. Let's face it, a man will only shower you with so much money before he starts wanting more than your company in return. (And who can blame him?) Sadly, that's the nature of the beast. Stripping is all about the art of the tease and sooner or later, customers simply grow tired of getting teased. Granted, it takes some customers many months—and countless thousands of dollars—to get it through their thick heads that you'll never treat them to anything more than a *look* at your naked flesh. But they'll keep that dream alive, hoping someday you'll just cave in and actually go home with them. The key is not to push them away. Let them try and try and try until they just give up. With some, it's a long (and expensive) journey. However, on occasion dancers actually do buy into the "sugar daddy" or "kept woman" scenario, continuing the relationship with their oh-so-beneficial customers beyond the sanctity of the strip club. However, of all the stripper-customer relationships I've heard about, just about all of them ended quickly. And badly.

For instance, when one dancer's benefactor found out she was allowing her *real* boyfriend to spend most nights in an apartment he paid for, he had the electricity, cable, and telephone shut off within a matter of hours. And then there was the dancer who returned to her provided condo—only to find the wife of her provider ready and waiting for her.

Apparently, the wife had found the key to their little love nest and, while Ms. Thing was out getting her nails done, the furious spouse tore all the stripper's clothes to shreds. The guilty husband convinced the dancer not to press charges for property damage by paying her a pretty penny. Still, replacing her entire wardrobe—including some incredible outfits she had picked up in Europe during a brief modeling stint—was a devastating experience.

Some dancers actually go through a period of mourning when a big-tipping regular grows tired of the game and moves off in search of greener (and easier) pastures. Think about it—it's a serious blow when a hefty chunk of your steady income suddenly stops flowing in. But the dancer-regular customer relationship is a never-ending cycle. No sooner has one relationship ended when another starts anew.

I remember one wealthy guy, a restaurant owner who, over the period of seven months, wound up being a regular for five different dancers in the same club, myself included. During that time, I'd say he spent close to $20,000 in all. And not once did he get one of us into bed. At least, if he did, I didn't hear about it. It's a harsh fact, I know, but some guys are just gluttons for punishment and thank God for that!

# 7

# Special Events

In addition to the standard offering of tits and ass, some clubs get creative and put on special events to attract attention or boost their draw on what might otherwise be slow nights. For these events, admission fees are always increased (usually doubled), but guys flock to the clubs in droves and the houses are usually packed.

Featured-dancer shows—put on by famous adult-magazine centerfolds or established or up-and-coming porn stars—are common to most clubs, but it's the multi-girl events, involving girls who already dance at the hosting club, that I'm referring to.

Foxy Boxing was one of my favorites. For this semi-violent form of entertainment—which makes *Celebrity Boxing* look like a love-fest—girls put on enormously oversized boxing gloves and "slug it out" with one another on the main stage in a makeshift ring. Some of the bouts are honest-to-goodness grudge matches, involving dancers who truly want (and try) to take each others' heads off. On the other hand, some fights start off as playful contests, only to escalate into serious altercations. At one club I worked, female customers were invited to join the action. But after a brutish lesbian biker chick took out one of the establishment's top-earning dancers just seconds into the first round, that policy was quickly abandoned. I never took part in the faux-fisticuffs—I'm a shopper, not a fighter.

One of my favorite events was baby-oil wrestling. Not to participate in, mind you (I never did), but to watch the customers drooling and tripping over their tongues as the girls did their best WWE imitations in kiddie pools filled with a half-inch or so of baby oil. Mud-wrestling and jello-wrestling events were also well-received by the customers, although the girls aren't too fond of either. Mud wrestling is loathed for obvious reasons—what it does to recent manicures, pedicures, and hair-stylings is akin to lighting hard-earned money on fire—and often the clubs have to reimburse the girls for their self-pampering expenditures. But at least the mud has a positive effect on the skin. Strangely, jello wrestling is more hated than its dirt-and-water counterpart. Many of the girls claim the sugary substance has a bleaching effect on their hair. Personally, I never suffered any problems with my locks as a result of contact with the quivering dessert, but I had other qualms: I've always had a bit of a sweet tooth and the jello nights usually induced a calorie craving that only a box of chocolate donuts would cure.

While the special-event nights are great for the house—lots of people paying steeper cover charges and drinking plenty of liquor—the dancers usually wind up getting the raw end of the deal. Customers receive hours of entertainment for roughly the price of one VIP Room lap dance. Getting them to part with more of their cash after the show is over is like pulling teeth. Fortunately, the alcohol flows like a river after the thaw and persistence usually pays off.

On event nights, the clubs pay a bonus to the girls who participate, and for some—especially those who aren't go-getters—the extra money is a real gift, but the majority of the dancers I knew would prefer to take their chances solo in the VIP Room. Finding a big spender just doesn't happen while rolling around in a tub of mud.

Participation in these events isn't mandatory—at least not in the clubs I worked in—but unless enough girls take part to make a show, they don't take place. Personally, I thought they were prime opportunities for the lazy girls, dancers who didn't have the personality, or the skill, to ring the bell on their own. Every club has its fair share, just as all jobs do.

Clean-up after a messy event isn't a problem—provided the club has a shower. Some do, some don't. Of the clubs that did, I remember one nasty wash-down facility that made a poorly funded homeless shelter's shower look sterile.

Again, I never took part in any of these events. Call me a party pooper, but it wasn't worth the risk. Cut a lip, chip a tooth, break your nose, any injury that marred your face would easily result in a loss of income, possibly for a long time. While I never saw or heard about any of the dancers getting seriously banged up—to the extent that they missed more than a day or two of work—I wasn't about to roll the bones, especially not my own.

# 8

## Lessons Learned

*E*veryone makes mistakes. At work, at play, in life—they're unavoidable. And during my topless career, I made my fair share. However, I was fortunate never to make any blunders serious enough to have had a detrimental effect on me. But I learned something from each and every one of the occasional bumps in the road and I used those errors as stepping stones—to improve not only my topless dancing, but also my life outside the club.

One of the first mistakes I made while dancing had to do with a fear I had prior to the start of my topless career. I knew I'd eventually encounter someone at the club who knew me outside the exotic entertainment industry. It was just a matter of when. Well, it happened about four months into my new profession. I'd just finished a table dance and was heading out for a cigarette break when a guy grabbed my hand and asked me to take him back to the VIP Room for a dance. Knowing the extra money would help me more than the nicotine, I quickly agreed and, without even looking at him, led him to the back room. As soon as we got inside and I got a good look at him, I realized the mammoth error I'd made.

Jack, as I'll refer to him in this story, was a close friend of my parents. Just two weeks earlier, I'd joined his wife, my parents, and him for a nice dinner out. Had I taken the time to look him in the eye while we were out in the club, perhaps I would have been able to ditch him and make my escape before he recognized me. But in my haste, I treated him like just another anonymous living wallet.

Standing there face to face in the better lighting of the VIP Room, I'm sure I looked whiter than an albino polar bear in a blizzard. I was certain he would recognize me at any moment and I had no idea what to do or say when it happened. Amazingly, it never did. Perhaps he'd had one cocktail too many—although he didn't seem to be drunk—or maybe his mind just refused to make the connection, but after a few minutes had passed it became clear to me that he didn't have a clue who I was. And if his lack of acuity wasn't proof enough, what he said next confirmed it.

Instead of asking me to dance, he asked me if I needed a place to live. Despite the fact that he was married, which he willingly volunteered (and I already knew), Jack suggested he rent a great apartment or condo for me so he could come over and visit "every now and then." Rather than clue him in as to who I was, I let him continue digging himself a hole—although it was starting to become a grave.

Jack confided in me that he'd been unhappy in his marriage for years and that he'd done everything to make it work, but his love spark was long gone. He said he hadn't yet had an affair—I didn't know what to believe from this guy—though he'd thought about it for years; he just couldn't get up the courage to act on it. Once again, I didn't know if this was the truth or just some weird bad-guy good-guy sadsack pick-up line.

Jack continued trying to woo me into becoming his kept woman, telling me that he had watched me dance for a few people that night and he just knew I was the right girl for him. He said he felt we had chemistry together, despite the fact that we'd never met before. Yeesh! He offered me a car, new clothes, endless nights on the town; basically, anything my heart desired and more. He told me he owned his own business (true) and said he had plenty of money to keep me in high style (also true). I'd never been out on his sailboat, but according to my folks, he had a nice one.

Of course, Jack could have had more money than the Sultan of Brunei and I wouldn't have considered being his mistress—or anyone's mistress, for that matter. It was just so weird hearing him say all these things when he and his wife appeared to be such a happy couple. I guess you never really know, do you?

Unable to listen to any more of his come-ons, I grabbed him by the shoulders and told him to forget about his fantasy scenario. I said I thought he ought to go home to his wife and try to work things out. Take her on a great vacation and try to reconnect with her. I reasoned with him that if he truly hadn't cheated on her yet, then maybe he didn't really want to. Maybe he was just confused. Now, I'm no marriage counselor, but I felt I had to say something. The ball was in my court; I figured the least I could do was take a swing at it.

Jack tried to change the subject and get me to dance for him, but by then I desperately needed a cigarette—hell, I needed the whole pack—along with a good stiff drink. I walked him back through the club and to the door, then had one of the bouncers escort him to his car, telling them not to let him back in. At first, Jack tried to put up a fight, but I kissed him on the cheek and told him to go home. My soft-spoken advice, coupled with the doorman's menacing stare, did the trick and he nodded his agreement. He also gave me a $50 tip before he split, an unexpected bonus that I considered appropriate for my good marital-counseling deed.

For a month after the incident, I considered whether or not I should talk to his wife, or at least write her an anonymous letter, letting her in on the secret I'd become privy to. In the end I decided to do nothing. Their marriage was none of my business and, although I would have hated to see her get hurt, maybe she was doing the exact same thing. Incidentally, Jack never came into the club again and he and his wife are still married. Happily? Who knows?

From that night on, I never blindly accepted someone's lap, table, or VIP Room dance offer without giving him a thorough once-over. This self-promise could wind up saving my hide in more ways than one and I'd be damned if I were going to make the same mistake twice. Fortunately, luck was with me that night and my private life remained just that.

And speaking of promises, at the start of my career in adult entertainment, I promised myself that I'd never date anyone from one of the clubs I worked at—customers or employees alike. Sad to say, I broke both of those vows.

You already know about my ill-fated dinner with the budget-minded meat-loving doorman. My other big strip club dating mistake was with a guy who came in as part of a bachelor-party crew. Handsome and muscular with a great smile, I was attracted to Mike the second I saw him. After two lap dances, I could tell the feeling was mutual. Before he left, we exchanged numbers—his cell, my phone service— and a few days later we hooked up.

We did dinner and a movie on the first date and he was a perfect gentleman. Other than a playful kiss goodnight, he didn't try anything too aggressive and I had the feeling that this relationship, if that's what it evolved into, had potential. But five weeks and a host of dates later, I found out the inside scoop and I was disgusted. Another dancer I was friendly with was dating one of Mike's buddies. Drunk one night, the friend let the cat out of the bag about how Mike was always bragging about how cool he was for having a stripper for a trophy girlfriend, the kind of girl you fooled around with, but never brought home to mom or, God forbid, married.

So one night after dinner and drinks, just when Mike thought he was going to get lucky, I hit him with the full brunt of the conversation. At first, he denied the statements, but when he realized that I wasn't going to buy the denial, he tried to explain them away as a simple misunderstanding. I cut him off in mid-sentence; I'd heard enough from him and his appeal to me was now long gone. After ripping him a new asshole for what he thought he knew about my character, I turned my back on him and ended the brief tryst for good. A few weeks later Mike came back into the club with the hopes of patching things up. I turned him down, he left, and I never heard from him again.

Mike is just one of the many guys out there who look upon strippers as easy. They figure that girls who work in the sex business are nymphos with loose morals ready and willing to climb into bed with any and every man who shows them the time of day. It's the most ridiculous belief about the industry. In fact, it seemed to me that most of the women in the profession were less apt to give it up than girls who worked in more "respected" occupations. (Watch out for those dental hygienists—they're real sexpots!)

After ending it with Mike, I became extremely guarded with my social life. Not only did I not date another customer or employee from the clubs, but I became overly critical of the men I did go out with. I was already ridiculously picky before my immersion in the world of topless dancing. Now, I'd turned into a perfectionist. I viewed all the men who were interested in me—even those outside the clubs—as wanting me for the wrong reasons and I refused to allow myself to get close to them. Stripping elevated me to a position of power over men, a commonality shared by nearly every female exotic entertainer, and to become someone's girlfriend, for lack of a better term, especially in our male-dominant society, was too alien a concept to consider. It was for that reason that my social life became essentially nonexistent for nearly three years. Sure, I dated on and off, but whenever I thought we were getting too close—SNAP!—the relationship, what little there was of it, was over.

It took me a long time to reconcile the difference between the men inside and outside the clubs. Even after I was finished with topless dancing, warming up to potential suitors, just for a simple date or two, wasn't easy. I still viewed the opposite sex as a paycheck—and I was far from a money-hungry user—but breaking out of that mindset was no simple task.

Abstaining from drinking while I danced was another self-imposed rule that I violated. I always wanted to be clear-minded and level-headed when I worked and, because my tolerance for alcohol is no greater than a hummingbird's, I figured it best if I limited my cocktail consumption to one or two per night, if that. But after a few years of strutting my stuff, I began to throw caution to the wind and let my hair down a little. It was a mistake that could have cost me.

One night, I had a pretty wicked buzz on. I wasn't falling-down drunk or making a fool of myself, but I was clearly not my normal self. I had flown to another city to work in a happening club for a few days, so I was unfamiliar with the other employees. When a bouncer offered to drive me back to my hotel after work, I happily agreed to let him take me.

The drive from the hotel to the club was a mere 10 minutes. His roundabout route took nearly half an hour—and there was no traffic. Throughout the ride, he pestered me to let him take me home to his place. Intoxicated as I was, I was firm in my refusal. Problem was, with his size—a gargantuan six-feet-plus and nearly 300 pounds—and my less-than-sharp condition, had he decided to press the issue, chances are I would have been in deep deep trouble. Fortunately, his aggressiveness was limited to verbal come-ons and I eventually made it back to my hotel unscathed. But the next morning, when my head cleared, I kicked myself for being so stupid. Never again in my topless career did I allow myself to venture outside of my sobriety comfort zone. It just wasn't worth the risk.

That night's events—and the thought of what *may* have happened—caused me to tell my mother what I was doing, although I didn't exactly confess the whole truth. I said I was waiting tables in a bikini bar to pick up some extra cash. She didn't have a problem with that. But about a year into the lie I came totally clean. To my amazement she supported my decision. Granted, she wasn't overly enthused about my career move, but she respected my judgment and didn't try to get me to quit. I promised myself that I'd never give her a reason to regret allowing me to choose my own path.

# 9

# More Bang for Your Bucks

Because I'm no longer trying to fleece horny customers out of their cash, I can safely slide to your side of the table (dance) and pass along some inside information that will not only enhance those visits to your favorite jiggle joint the next time you go, but help you get more bang for your buck—perhaps even literally.

Once you've decided to blow off the dinner-and-a-movie you'd thought about with your significant other in favor of a night out with the guys, and your posse has voted unanimously to spend the evening eyeballing fresh T & A in an up-close-and-personal environment, a decision needs to be made. Will it be boobs and thongs or the full monty? Now, this might sound like an arbitrary decision, but if you're at all interested in imbibing, consider the fact that most all-nude clubs do not serve alcohol. Something to do with the law, I believe. And a club without a liquor license definitely needs to offer something extra special to bring people in, hence the bottomless policy.

Another important item that should factor into your decision is the quality of the women you want to view. In most major cities, topless clubs have more attractive girls than their totally bare competitors. I think it's a simple case of class; most all-nude clubs have none. They tend to be on the sleazier side and the top-earning strippers will avoid those establishments like the plague. However, major markets such as New York, Dallas, Los Angeles, Atlanta, Chicago, and Miami usually have at least one full snog bar with quality babes.

Before journeying to the club of choice, consider how you're going to get there. First impressions are extremely important, especially at ritzy clubs with valet services. Word quickly spreads to the girls inside—via the doorman or the house-mom—about the car you arrive in. And if you're even considering leaving with one of the dancers (your chances are remote, but anything is possible), you'd better have a horse-drawn carriage and not a pumpkin with wheels! If you're going with a group and everyone plans on drinking, rent a limo. Not only do they convey a sense of wealth, but if there's a line waiting to get in, perhaps the doorman will mistake you for someone of importance and allow you to cut it. If all else fails, at least you can drink till you drown and not worry about a tree jumping in front of you on the way home.

On the other hand, if you're going by yourself, avoid the limo treatment at all costs. Guys flying solo and arriving via chauffeur have a tendency to look like stalkers and preda-tors. You'd be much better off handing the valet attendant the keys to a racy Ferrari, Lamborghini, or similar exotic car. And even if you don't own one, these days you can rent one for less than what a limo would cost you for the night. Trust me on this one, most dancers worthy of your atten-tion have been in limousines before—but very few of them have ridden in Ferraris.

Before you enter the club, consider the monster-sized slab of meat with eyes standing before you who conveys without words that laying a finger on one of *his* girls will result in *your* leaving in a body bag. These guys are usually paid an hourly wage and have an affinity for violence. Face it, they're not there to solve complex mathematical equations! When all is said and done, you absolutely want this guy on your side. My suggestion: Tip the sonofabitch. A fiver if you're alone ought to do the trick, a sawbuck or double sawbuck if you're with a group. Should a "touching encounter" occur inside the club, even if it's a harmless and completely accidental brushing, your initial act of benevolence may just save your ass. In the past, broken arms have been miraculously avoided in favor of a few harsh words, courtesy of a few bucks up front.

Believe me, the bouncers view themselves along the same lines as Secret Service agents guarding governmental bigwigs and they always err on the side of caution, taking a dancer's word over a customer's about an incident that allegedly occurred. Translated: They will forcibly remove someone first and ask questions later. Far beyond just an ego stroke with these guys, making an example of someone crossing the line sends out a powerful message to the rest of the customers, especially those Yellow Pages readers who let their fingers do the walking.

Once, this guy was in the club no more than five minutes when he spanked the ass of a dancer walking up onto the stage. Seconds later, he was doing an impressive imitation of a javelin, although his eventual touch-down in the parking lot was far from clean and quiet. Another time, an overly amorous (and inebriated) regular decided that $500 in lap dances and tips deserved more than just a peck on the cheek. He latched on to the stripper like a lamprey eel, intent on getting his money's worth. Her cries for help summoned the nearest leg-breaker and a python-like chokehold changed the man's tune in an instant. By the time he was dragged to the door he was completely unconscious. They almost had to call an ambulance for that guy, but a bucket of cold water did the trick. Those examples aside, for the most part minor customer-dancer infractions are resolved without violence. No one will come to a slaughterhouse; successful clubs are all about sex and fantasy, not violence and destruction.

In addition to getting on his good side, tipping the doorman can provide a bounty of information, such as which girls give the best dances. You could also ask him if the VIP Room is *anything goes*, but that might just set off his alarm bells and trigger his smash-your-face response. So be cool with what you say; you're much better off waiting to pop that question inside. At the very least, the tip should help him remember you and guarantee better treatment on your next visit. For that same reason, slip him $5 on the way out.

Once you're inside, you have two choices of where to sit: at the bar or at a table. If it's your first time at the club or if you just want to get the feel of the place, take a seat at the bar. Dancers are less likely to pester you for lap dances there and you'll get the opportunity to survey the scene from afar. Be careful what you order, though, because at some clubs, where draft brews can cost upwards of $7, a multi-ingredient mixed drink might break your bankroll. Remember, you can drink all you want at home—save your money for all of those gorgeous babes you don't routinely find in your living room. Along those same lines, if you're trying to save money, you can do your drinking prior, but if you're *too* wasted, the doorman might not let you in.

So let's say you take a seat at the bar and the resident mixologist immediately asks you if you'd like to buy the beautiful half-naked girl—the beautiful half-naked girl who just *sidled up beside you*—a drink. Before you say yes, do yourself a favor by putting your hormones on hold and finding out what the little miss is drinking first. Otherwise, there's a damn good chance you'll hear the pop! of a champagne cork, the fizz! of the bubbles, and the sinking! of your heart as the bartender pleasantly informs you that you're now the proud owner of a $400 bottle of Cristal.

One time, the above scenario occurred nearly to the letter, except it was *two* bottles! The poor schmuck had to settle his tab with a credit card, a debit card, and all of his on-hand cash. With no remaining *dinero,* the dancers treated him like a leper at a nudist colony—after the bottles were drained, of course.

The upside about strip clubs is that you don't have to worry about drink minimums—most of the better clubs simply don't have them. Believe me, they have other ways of getting your money without bankrupting you on booze.

Which brings to mind the flower girl. Usually only found in the classier strip clubs—if there is such a thing—flower girls flit around with a basket of roses, oftentimes selling one for the same price as a rose *garden.* Most of the flower girls would rather be dancers, but for some reason—problems with nudity, little confidence in their bodies, or a lack of dancing ability—they opt to stay clothed and make the rounds like semi-sexy candy stripers. When you see a flower girl coming, alarm bells should start going off. Make sure you put a lock on your wallet and prepare to say: "No." Guys buying and giving these botanical pretties to the bare-breasted beauties expecting special treatment in return are sadly mistaken. In fact, on numerous occasions, after the rose-giver has gone home, the rose gets recycled … right back into the basket from which it came.

As for the aforementioned resident mixologist, if the strip club were a major literary work on which you were to be tested, the bartender is, without question, your booklet of Cliff Notes. Drink-slingers are privy to anything and everything that happens inside their establishment. Whether it takes place at the bar, on center stage, in the lavatory, or in the VIP Room, chances are the bartender has the scoop. Tip that man (or woman) well and the club will soon be *your* oyster, offering up its precious pearl.

Cocktail waitresses are a hit-or-miss affair. Some are cordial and pleasant, happy to serve you and cater to your every beck and call. Others are invisibly stoop-shouldered, the result of that burdensome chip they carry as a result of being denied stripper status. That's not to say all cocktail waitresses aspire to be dancers, but in an upscale topless club the nightly take-home-pay differential between the two positions is like molehills and mountains.

Understanding how the stage (or stages) works is an important aspect of your strip club experience. Most clubs require all the dancers to take a turn on the stage. The stage rotation is a great opportunity for guys to sample the goods without having to shell out a lot of coin. Whatever you do, don't throw your big bills away here. Save them for more intimate encounters, such as table and lap dances or the VIP Room. For the stage, singles are fine, fives if you think she's really worth it. A good trick is to keep your bigger bills ($20s, $50s, $100s) on the outside of your money wad. Sometimes, girls think they're getting more than they really are—especially if you crumple them up before you throw them—and they might give you an extra wiggle, shake, or spread. Also, never leave your money out by your drink. I used to crawl to the end of the stage, pull a bill from a guy's stack, crumple it, and sexily blow it on stage toward my pile. I'd start small, with his Washingtons or Lincolns; then, when the guy was captivated by my blowing technique, I'd go for his *big* bills. Dancers generally make the least amount of their money on stage, but one night I pocketed more than $500 during a set (two songs)—from one guy, no less.

Lap dances, lap dances, lap dances … As defined by Webster (and not that little black kid on TV!), a "lap dance" is a dance that takes place a foot in front of you, lasts the duration of a song, and has no touching by either party whatsoever.

Now, in the real world, depending on the girl, a lap dance may involve the brush of a breast, the grind of a butt, a knee meeting an inner thigh, and so on. Truth is, most of the girls do *a lot* of touching. Guys usually won't shell out the heavy coin if they don't get to sample the goods, at least to some degree. Think about it: Would you buy a car without test-driving it first?

At some clubs, however, management gives the girls free reign to do whatever the heck they want. I quit working in one Sin City strip joint because I refused to prostitute myself like some other girls; blowjobs in the VIP Room were a frequent occurrence.

Lap dances range anywhere from $10 to whatever a girl thinks she can get away with. The most I ever charged was $150 a dance, but the circumstances surrounding that night were special: The customer was wealthy, drunk, and celebrating a divorce. Basically, he was ripe for the taking.

A good rule of thumb is to find out at the door, or at the bar, how much a lap dance costs. Also, make sure you tell the dancer exactly how many lap dances you want. Often, I linked one with another and another and before the guy knew it, he owed me for five. Keep in mind that if there's a dispute over nonpayment for services rendered, the house almost always sides with the girl and the guy is often asked to leave—sometimes ass over teakettles—after the dispute (and the tab) has been settled. If a guy has friends with him, there's a damn good chance *they* might get charged for tits and ass they never even got to see! The bottom line: Someone is always counting. More important, someone will definitely be *paying*.

And then there's the infamous VIP Room. Quite simply, this is a more intimate setting where management doesn't pay attention (in theory) and the dancers can get away with more—if they want to. It's usually one-on-one and dances *always* cost more. People often ask if guys really get laid in the VIP Room. While I can't speak for anyone else, I know I never prostituted myself inside (or out of) a strip club. But I'm sure it happens. Stories circulate and rumors abound. (The Gold Club in Atlanta received a ton of attention regarding this issue; club workers testified that many top NBA players received *special* treatment.) Of course, it really all depends on what girl is back there with the customers. But I'll tell you this much, if Charlie Sheen didn't get Scooby Snacks after dropping fifty large one night at Scores in New York, he deserves a full refund. The old adage, "You get what you pay for," can be applied here, but keep in mind that prostitution is illegal in most places and, as the bee said to the beekeeper, "Stings happen!"

Assuming you're not a member of the franks-n-beans club, that doesn't mean you're not welcome in a strip club. Quite the contrary. Men, women, straight, gay, transvestites, transsexuals, hell, even Transylvanians for that matter … if you've got the greens, then you've got the means. Nor does a woman have to be a lesbian to admire a dancer at work. Nowadays, lots of women come in with their guy friends and have an awesome time. (That's what started it all for me.) Girls generally don't mind dancing for girls—and the guys really get off on watching. Also, if the guys are a bit handsy to begin with, having a chick in their posse might cause them to cool their jets, a scenario most dancers greatly appreciate. (My friendship with Jennifer and Rebecca began that way.) Plus, women have the advantage of avoiding the club's cover charge by telling the doorman that they're interested in dancing there. This ploy usually works only once, so make it count.

So you came, you saw, and now you want to conquer. Hang on right there, bub. Picking up the strippers ain't easy.

We dance because we want *money*, not dates. We can get more dates than fifty Arabs standing under a forest of palm trees during a windstorm. Unless you're a well-known celebrity entertainer or sports superstar, you've got strikes against you right off the bat. Again, if you don't meet the above criteria, here are a few suggestions.

First and foremost, go with a group of friends. Guy's night out, bachelor party, frat party—you name it. Contrary to popular belief, if you show up alone, dancers probably tag you as someone on the hunt or a spooky stalker with questionable motives. The same can be said of regulars. Guys who show up night after night, while admired for their financial contributions to the cause, are almost never considered as relationship material—unless it's for sugar-daddy purposes. If you're cute, in good shape, and have a smashing personality, there's a chance you might sneak in under the radar. A big bank account won't hurt your chances, either. But if you come off as desperate, forget about it.

Second, make sure you dress the part. Mustard-stained bowling shirts won't cut it. Only guys like Russell Crowe and Brad Pitt can get away with tattered jeans and a ripped flannel. Armani speaks volumes, as do Hugo Boss and Christian Dior. Casual dress is fine, too, provided it's in style. But don't be too casual (jeans and a black T-shirt are fine), otherwise you'll look as if you rushed to get there with no regard for your personal appearance. Loosely translated in dancer-speak, that equals a big fat "L" on your forehead, visible only to the strippers. And speaking of T-shirts, don't ever wear a T-shirt bearing that club's, or any other strip club's, logo. Once again, you'll look like a total idiot and definitely not someone one of the dancers would want to go home with. As far as jewelry is concerned, unless you're a rock star—a *real* rock star—with a platinum album and a pack of groupies, stick to a nice watch and one or, at the most, two rings. Looking like a pawnbroker or a pimp won't score you any bonus points. And if you decide to wrap a Rolex around your wrist, make damn sure the secondhand sweeps. Believe me, dancers know what's real and what isn't— I don't care how good your knock-off looks.

In terms of your occupation, unless it's a profession with a serious wow-factor—Navy SEAL, astronaut, race-car driver, brain surgeon—you might be better off staying silent. Of course, you could always lie. Try printing up some business cards advertising yourself as a movie producer or a theatrical agent (but beware of looking like a glam scammer). Even if you're not in *the industry*, many of the dancers are wanna-be actresses and models and are always looking for that big break. And never use your home number; set up a voice-mail with your fictitious company's name. At the very least, your wife won't catch you in the act.

On the flip side, be wary when a dancer gives you her telephone number. Chances are she's just trying to string you along for more cash. You might want to bring a cell phone into the club and call from the bathroom. But even if you do get her voice, it's possible she set up a dummy voicemail, too.

Of course, phone numbers aren't the only things dancers lie about. Those crazy names you thought they were born with are used for their protection. I know a guy who dated a dancer for six months before he found out her real name. Whatever you do, don't press a dancer for her true identity. If she wants to tell you, she will. Otherwise, go along with the charade. Keep pushing her to reveal herself, however, and any chance you had of actually breaking through her defenses will be gone before you know it.

Beyond that, play it cool and try not to be too much of a dog—at least, not in her presence. With topless dancers, the hard-to-get routine definitely pays greater dividends than the frequent flier. Show all your cards right off the bat and the poker game is over—and believe me, babe, you *lost* the pot. You shouldn't come across as too desperate or too anxious, and you definitely shouldn't make the strip club your second home. Go once a week, at most, but better yet, try starting off by going once every two weeks. As I've said before, once you've been tagged as a return customer, you're done. The hook's been set and now all she has to do is reel you in. Just like in life, less can definitely be more. But don't think that you can *look* the part of a real player while tipping like a miser—or worse—and still curry good favor with the hopes that you'll eventually loosen the strings on your wallet. Nice try, pal, but that ploy won't work. Whether you look the part or not, cash is still king in the strip club. And if you're truly loaded like Fort Knox, your best bet is to follow the Chunky's Soup commercial's mantra, "More is good."

Aside from that, all I can offer you is a hearty good luck. You'll need it.

# Part Two

## Tales From the VIP Room

# 10

# The VIP Room

*A*h, the VIP Room. Nearly every strip club has one and each has its own personality. Some have cozy wrap-around couches, some are fully mirrored, some have poles and mini-stages, and one even had a Jacuzzi tub built for two. Some are brightly lit, some are dim and hazy, and some are darker than the blackest cave. Some have music blaring, some are noticeably quieter, and some have no speakers at all. But regardless of their interior characteristics, all are designed to allow for more personal interaction and intimacy between a customer and the dancer, or dancers, of his/her choosing. Of course, this one-on-one (or two-on-one or twenty-on-one) attention comes at a price: Lap dances—customers usually expect a whole lot more than that—in the VIP Room are often double (and then some) what a lap dance costs in the main club. And it's here that the wildest, craziest, most unimaginable situations occur.

All the stories you're about to read are true. Most were witnessed first-hand; the rest were relayed to me by co-workers. Some are hard to believe. Some are nearly *impossible* to believe. But if you saw what I saw on a daily basis, you'd have concrete proof that truth is stranger than fiction.

The door to the VIP Room is now open. Enter if you dare.

# 11

# The "Pit" Boss

*L*et me make one thing perfectly clear—this story has absolutely *nothing* to do with casinos. I'd been working at a seedy club in a major city for about a week, finishing my turn on stage, when a good-looking middle-aged gentleman—he looked like a doctor or a lawyer—said he wanted to go to the VIP Room with me. I smiled, took his hand, and started to lead him back there. En route, Cinnamon, a long-legged redhead and veteran of the club, sidled up beside me and whispered something to the effect of: "You're gonna have fun with this guy, but I hope you're wearing deodorant." She giggled and pranced away, leaving me clueless as to what the hell she was talking about.

We got to the VIP Room and after I told him my rate and he agreed, I got down to business. But just as I started to dance, he shook his head "No" and whipped out a small Polaroid camera, one of those older folding models.

"Do you mind if I take a picture?" he asked.

"Not at all," I replied. "But it'll cost you."

"Certainly," he said with a smile.

But before I could tell him my fee was $20, he produced a wad of cash and peeled off a $100. Greedily, I snatched up the crisp bill and struck my sexiest pose. Strangely, the guy frowned.

"That's nice, but not what I want."

I was confused. "What *do* you want?"

"Come closer, and lift up your arm."

"Huh?"

"Your arm," he pointed. "Lift it up. I want to see that beautiful pit."

At first, I thought he was kidding. But when I saw that he wasn't, I nearly burst out laughing. Quickly, I came to my senses. After all, no matter how you slice it, a hundred dollars is still a hundred dollars. So I did as he asked and let him snap the photo of my smooth hairless armpit.

The guy smiled like a kid in a candy store, stepped closer, aimed, and took the picture.

When the photograph was fully developed, he kissed it. "Beautiful," he said lustily. "Now, I need your scent."

This guy was starting to freak me out. "What do you mean, my *scent*?"

Once again, he pointed to my armpit. "I have to wipe this against you to capture your essence."

I couldn't believe this was happening. I wanted to kick Cinnamon for not fully explaining this guy's antics. Seeing that I was uncomfortable, the guy took out his money roll and peeled off another hundred.

"Will this help?" he said. My arm went up faster than a little kid in a classroom who knows the answer to an easy question.

When he was done wiping the photograph on my armpit, he took out a small plastic baggie and secured the picture inside it as if he were a Crime Scene Investigator collecting evidence. Then he proceeded to bargain me down to fifty bucks for the other armpit. The guy must've been in sales! When he was finished, he packed up the photos, put away the camera, took my hand in his, and kissed it.

"Thank you," he said. "I'll cherish these forever."

Yeah, right, I thought. Whatever works for you. Yeesh!

After he left, I tracked down Cinnamon in the dressing room. By then, she'd told a few of the other girls what was going on.

"Welcome to the club," one of the girls said. "He's already gotten all of us."

Apparently, the guy had been coming to the club for more than a year and had already "pitted" all the veteran dancers. Now, each time he came in, he zeroed in on the new talent.

I'm afraid to think what he does with the photos in the privacy of his own home. I'm just glad I shaved before going to work that night.

# 12

## The Exterminator

While this whole crush fetish thing—stomping insects and other small critters to death for voyeuristic jollies—is the latest rage, I know a dancer who experienced it first-hand (actually, first-*foot)* years before it became, uh, popular.

Princess was doing her thing in the VIP Room when her customer whipped out a small plastic film canister and asked her if she wanted to "stomp some bugs for bucks."

Princess turned green at the suggestion, but quickly reconsidered when he offered to pay her on a per-bug basis. They eventually agreed on $10 each, a hefty sum in the insect-bashing biz.

The guy opened the canister and dumped out a small pile of skinny yellowish-brown mealworms. (Princess described them to us later; one of the girls had a pet chameleon and knew exactly what they were.)

Princess got brave, spread the pile of worms out with the point of her high heel, counted 32, and asked to see the

$320 before she raised a foot.

He flashed, she smashed. Nauseous as she was, the money worked better than a bottle of Pepto Bismol. However, she did throw away her $49 pair of stilettos after the stomp-fest was over.

About a week went by before the "Exterminator"—that's what Princess nicknamed him—returned. Once again, he asked her to join him in the VIP Room. This time, he had a Tupperware container filled with cockroaches—27 to be precise.

Princess could feel the bile rising in her stomach, but when the Exterminator offered $25 per bug, she couldn't turn him down. She did the deed, pocketed the $675, and hurried to the bathroom where she promptly re-tasted her lunch. She also tossed her shoes—another pair of $49 stilettos—and took the rest of the night off.

Over the next month, the Exterminator made three more appearances at the club, each time bringing a new container of bugs—spiders, crickets, and earthworms—and selected Princess to do the stomach-turning tap dance. Although the floor of the VIP Room was littered with broken bug bodies and guts after each stampede, the money was just too good to pass up and Princess tipped one of the doormen $50 to clean up after each grisly occasion.

However, when the Exterminator showed up with a small box of baby white mice, Princess threw in the towel and had the guy escorted off the premises.

Seeing as how Princess was now experienced in the art of pest control, whenever one of the dancers spotted a roach or any other type of bug in the club, she was the first one we called and she never let us down.

# 13

## Sweet Feet

*I* was dancing for one of my regulars in the VIP Room at a club in Las Vegas when he propositioned me. The guy asked, flat out, if I wanted to earn some *real* money, and *not* by dancing.

With an icy stare, I told him I didn't play those games and that he should pay a visit to one of the state's legal brothels to scratch his itch. I grabbed my cover-up and started to leave when he began apologizing up and down, explaining that I took his proposition wrong and that sexual favors were not what he had in mind.

"Exactly what did you mean?" I asked testily.

The guy produced a couple of individual-serving-size jelly packets and a plastic butter knife. "I was hoping you'd let me spread this on your feet," he said matter-of-factly, as if it were the most ordinary thing in the world.

"What happens after you spread it on?"

"Well, I lick it off, of course," he replied quickly, before adding: "That is, if it's okay with you."

I'd been dancing close to four hours at that point, and I don't even want to think what my feet might have smelled like. If this lonely fetishy schlub wanted to spread strawberry preserves on my feet and then lick it off, hell, more power to him.

"How much money are we talking about?"

"Two hundred. Two-fifty if you'll let me spread it between your toes."

"Not interested," I said. "For that amount, I won't even let you *sniff* my feet, let alone lick them." Once again, I made a show of leaving, but as I hoped he would, he halted my progress.

"Okay, three-fifty. That's all I've got with me." He took out the money and offered it to me. "Please."

Truth is, I would have done it for his initial offer, but I had to try and up the score. After all, what he was proposing had to constitute oral sex in some states. And I do have pretty feet. Anyway, I snatched the cash, sat down on the couch, and popped off my heels.

"Go for it," I said. "But I'm only giving you two songs. If you're not done by then, I'm outta here, jelly and all."

The guy was on his knees and at my feet a split-second later. Come to think of it, that's how all men should be in my presence. The jelly felt really strange going on, but I pretended I was at the luxurious spa at one of Vegas' many hotels, treating myself to a foot massage and pedicure—something I would definitely be doing with *his* money the very next day.

When he began licking the jelly off, it felt weirder still, but the song was winding to a close, and I was too busy deciding what else I was going to be doing with the extra money to really care about what was happening to my little piggies. So long as he didn't try to gnaw off one of my toes, I could live with my decision.

In his defense, I have to say that not even a smudge of

jelly remained on my feet when the song ended, although I did find a strawberry seed under my big toenail in the bathtub later that night.

This routine was repeated nearly a dozen times while I worked at that club. The guy went through a host of flavors—apple, strawberry, and black currant, to name a few. But after the little "seed incident," I confined him to just jelly—no more preserves!

# 14

# The Love Glove

*H*oney—a real skank of a dancer whose company I despised—and I were dancing in the VIP Room of a Texas club for a guy named Eric—tall, tan, good-looking, mid-30s, dressed like a golf pro (minus the spiked shoes). We'd done about three songs for Eric who, strangely, was only drinking soda, when he removed a crumpled golf glove from his pocket and asked us how much we would charge him to rub it against our coochies.

Now, had Eric been drunk, I would have just laughed it off and continued to run up his dance tab, but the fact that he was stone-cold sober nearly caused me to slap him across the face. But Honey—who probably carried a pair of knee pads in her purse—plopped herself down on his lap, ran her fingers through his hair, and asked him what the deal was.

Eric claimed to be a professional golfer in the midst of a tournament in which he was close to the lead. According to him, he needed an extra *stroke* of good luck on the last day of the tourney.

Disgusted by the thought, I wanted no part of the glove-crotch interaction. Honey, on the other hand, thought the idea to be sexy and even felt honored—this chick was warped—that he would appeal to her to help him win his tournament.

Morbidly curious, I stuck around to watch Honey earn her measly fifty bucks, which is what she agreed to do it for. Once he had given her the cash, she took his golf glove, pulled her g-string aside, and wiped the glove against her nasty-assed pouty lips. Thinking back, that old well-worn golf glove might just have been the *cleanest* thing those lips had touched in years!

Honey handed him back the glove and kissed him on the cheek for extra good luck. I just took my lap dance money, said goodbye with a roll of my eyes, and left the room.

Honey spent the rest of the night bragging to the other girls that she had "blessed" some big golf pro's glove and that when he won, he was going to come back and share some of his winnings with her.

Yeah, right!

Two days later, the other dancers and I waited for Honey to arrive so we could grab the newspaper's sports section from the bartender and see how her new beau had placed in his competition.

She gave us his last name, which he had apparently given her along with his phone number, and we checked the PGA results. Strangely, his name wasn't in there at all. Thinking he had lied to her, Honey got all pissed off and stormed out of the dressing room, amid much laughter and teasing by the other girls.

But I noticed another set of golf results—from something called the Nike Tour. (I later found out that this was for professional golfers who didn't qualify, or hadn't yet qualified, for the PGA Tour.) Anyway, I scanned the list of names and, sure enough, I came across Honey's guy … Only he was close to the *bottom* of the list. The "help" she provided had been anything but. Well, I guess the saying holds true: "Loose lips sink ships." And if that's really the case, Honey's crotch is the *Titanic* all over again!

# 15

# *You Snooze, You Lose!*

*C*ustomers should treat topless dancers with respect. Those who don't would be much better off staying home with a bottle of their favorite intoxicant and an adult video. Here's a story about a man who could've used this advice.

I was working at a club in Los Angeles, dancing in the VIP Room for a bald fat guy with more chins than a Chinese phone book. I was midway through the first song when he uttered the first of his nasty comments. Apparently, he thought I wasn't "glittery" enough. Many of the other dancers had sequins or sparkles in their outfits; that night, I was wearing black leather.

"Hey, you picked *me*," I replied. "If you want someone else, have at it."

"No," he said. "I'll keep you. You look a little sleazy and I like that. It reminds me of my ex-wife."

Now, dancers hear all kinds of comments from their customers—some flattering, some disgusting, and some downright insulting. Usually, we take everything in stride. Most of the guys are just unwinding or drunk or both, so I let this remark slide, chalking it up to booze and a bad day. But a few moments later, he lashed out again.

"Those are the ugliest shoes I've ever seen," he laughed.

My immediate response was to ask that fat bastard when was the last time he saw his own shoes, but I held my tongue. Booze and a bad day, I said to myself. Still, his insult really pissed me off. I was wearing a pair of $150 Pradas and I know they looked good. What the hell did he know about fashion? Had he been talking about food, I would have taken his word for it, but designer heels, no friggin' way!

By the end of the second song—and his third Long Island Iced Tea—he was really starting to get belligerent, finding fault with just about everything I did. I was considering grabbing a bouncer and having him tossed out of the club when his karma came back to bite him.

Somehow, Mr. Bald & Fat nodded off. The loud music playing in the background apparently made no difference— he was counting sheep like a shepherd. Now I was really pissed! How the hell could anyone—even a drunk—fall asleep during one of my performances?

I walked over and was about to rouse him from his slumber when I changed my mind. Instead, I vicked one of his cigarettes, sat down on the couch, and took a break. Of course, his meter was still running like a high-priced taxi waiting on its fare. When the cocktail waitress came in to fetch him another round, I ordered a glass of wine for me— on him, of course.

This scenario continued for the next six songs. And since his platinum Visa was already imprinted at the bar, porky Rip van Winkle unknowingly treated almost half of the girls working that night to a cocktail or two.

Eventually, I decided he'd been punished enough, although he probably wouldn't learn anything from the experience, having slept through it.

I woke Mr. Bald & Fat, who looked at me with the same pissy expression he wore before falling asleep, then matter-of-factly asked me how much he owed. With a straight face, I gave him the number—$185. The break-down of his charges: $40 for the two dances he was awake for, $120 for the six "dances" he slept through, and an extra $25 for the "pain and suffering" brought on by his rude comments.

He shrugged, handed me two hundred-dollar bills, and said: "Keep the change. You could use a new hairdo."

As he walked out, I wished I had milked it for another twenty songs—along with a nice take-out steak & lobster dinner from the Palm.

The guy waddled to the bar, never batted an eye when the bartender hit him with the huge tab, paid it, and left. I never saw him again.

# 16

## The Collector

During my topless tenure, I had numerous encounters with and heard countless stories about customers (men and women alike) who bargained with dancers to purchase their personal items—in some cases, *very* personal items—as souvenirs. For some, those seeking to purchase a lock of hair or a couple of sequins from an outfit or even a garter, the small seemingly harmless tokens would serve as mementos of a fun evening out. For others, those looking to buy personal effects no one in his right mind would ask for, the items were undoubtedly part of large collections—large *twisted* collections—indicating that the collector-in-question was a few fries short of a Happy Meal. I'm talking about worn-out stockings, pump (shoe) inserts, toenail clippings, used razors, used tissues, used tampons, broken acrylic nails, empty cans of feminine deodorant spray—the list goes on and on, getting progressively worse as it goes.

Most times, we sold the customers the items they wanted

for a modest fee. Occasionally, we had the prospective buyer tossed out, if he/she really creeped us out. Were we adding fuel to a potential serial killer's obsessive fire by selling the items? Or on the flip side, were we setting him off by denying access to our personal goods? I don't know. But all types of people go to the clubs and strippers aren't the hall monitors of society—we're just trying to make a living. If pervs wanted to buy our garbage, more power to them; we took their money.

Having said that, trinket-seekers were commonplace and most just became a blur in my memory. But one guy, a well-dressed smallish man who looked like a cross between Radar O'Riley (from the TV show "MASH") and popcorn magnate Orville Reddenbacher, I will never forget.

I was finishing my turn on stage in a Southern California club when this cute balding little man wearing a suit and bowtie asked me to dance for him in the VIP Room. With a seductive smile, I took him by the arm and led him to one of the private booths in the back.

After a couple of dances, he asked me to sit with him, have a drink, and chat. I was glad to rest a spell and readily took him up on the offer. One drink became two and somehow we got onto the subject of feet. Not just any feet, mind you, but *my* feet. He asked me a slew of questions about my trotters and told me so much about them that I thought he was a podiatrist. Turns out he had a major foot fetish. That's when he confessed that he wanted to buy my feet.

Thinking it was just the alcohol talking, I laughed it off, but he explained that he wanted to take impressions of my feet using some type of plaster.

The whole idea weirded me out, but he went on to explain that he could do it in the club—in the VIP Room. Of course, he would pay me for my time. He added that he didn't ask to buy just any girl's feet—only those that he deemed exceptional. So I agreed. He got all excited, hugged me with all the strength he could muster, and gave me an extra $50 tip.

Sure enough, the guy came back the next day. But the bouncer—an overprotective monstrous big brother-type—almost didn't let him in due to the small gym bag he carried. Customers aren't allowed to bring duffels, backpacks, or other bags into the club for obvious reasons—even if they're searched. But I smoothed things over with a $20. (I knew the foot freak would reimburse me big time.)

So Foot-Man came inside and, giddy as a sumo wrestler at an all-you-can-eat buffet, took my hand and led me back to the VIP Room. He sat me down, got down on his knees as if he were a shoe salesman, took off my heels, and proceeded to clean every last inch of my dogs with baby wipes. When they were clean enough to eat off of, he reached into his gym bag and removed a pair of Tupperware-like rectangular trays. He dumped a bag of yellowish-white powder into each tray and produced a gallon jug of distilled water, which he poured into one of the trays, stopping when it was half full. Slowly and methodically, he mixed the concoction until it began to thicken, looking vaguely similar to wet cement with an eggshell hue. If the Mafia was looking for a new cement shoemaker, this guy should be first on their list!

Gently, he guided my right foot into the mixture and, softly but firmly, held my ankle so that my foot didn't touch the bottom of the tray. The goo felt like cool wet rubber and was not altogether unpleasant—although it did feel weird between my toes. (I remember thinking that, when he was finished, I could have the jelly-licker come in and suck off the residue, thereby earning myself some extra cash!)

After about fifteen minutes, the substance had hardened enough so that I could remove my foot without damaging the impression. Once again, he cleaned my foot thoroughly with baby wipes, even though there was nothing clinging to it. Then, he repeated the process with my left foot. The whole procedure took about forty minutes, netting me $350 (10 songs at $25 per, plus a $100 tip) for sitting up to my ankles in goo.

After he'd packed up his gear and put away the impressions, he delicately kissed each of my feet on the sole, helped me back into my heels, and bid me a fond farewell.

About a month went by and in walked my little bowtie-wearing friend. I took him by the arm and started to lead him to the VIP Room, but he told me he couldn't stay. He said he only came by to show me something. He whipped out a color photo of the interior of his home—and his *collection*.

What I saw shocked me, but I had to give him credit for his artistic panache, even though it was sort of funky. More than fifty pairs of feet filled his living room: on the shelves, on the end tables, hanging from lamps, on the walls … You name the place and there were feet galore! And he'd taken the time to paint each foot in a litany of colors, doing incredible justice, I might add, to the toenails. His work was so impressive, I was thinking of hiring him the next time I needed a pedicure.

Then he pointed to one specific pair. Mine. Painted in solid metallic gold, with fire-engine-red toenails, they were sitting on a small stand next to the front door.

"Your feet are the first things I want my guests to see when they come over," he said. "They're my favorite pair and I'll cherish them forever."

Sadly, he didn't let me keep the picture, stating that his collection was way too personal to be shared by anyone other than his closest friends. But he went on to say that, perhaps one day in the near future, he would come back and, if I was willing, do another cast.

"I'm considering moving up to legs," he said sincerely.

But I never saw him again.

# 17

# The Piggy Bank

Men aren't the only ones who frequent strip clubs. Women go all the time. Some go because they're thinking of dancing and they want to size up the competition. Some go with their boyfriends or girlfriends. And some go just because they enjoy looking at women's bodies. But I'll never forget one woman—a mid-40s, pleasant-looking, unassuming mother of three—who went for an entirely different reason.

Janice was sitting in the front row by the stage, looking rather embarrassed, as if she truly didn't want to be there. Being the congenial and hospitable person that I am, I walked over to her and introduced myself. We talked for a few moments, then she asked me if there was somewhere more private we could go so that she could ask me a personal question. When she offered to pay me for my time—the magic words in any strip club—I accepted.

Although I had no idea what she was leading up to, I didn't get a bad vibe from her. I've always been a good judge of character and Janice struck me as a nice lady, nothing more. So I agreed to lend her my ear and led her into the VIP Room where we could chat more privately.

It took her a moment to work up the courage to pose her question. When she finally did, my jaw nearly hit the floor.

"Would you mind if I looked at your pussy?" Janice asked matter of factly.

After the initial shock wore off, I took a step back from her, still trying to contemplate exactly what she wanted from me—other than a peek at my snatch. Noticing my confusion, she immediately elaborated on her question.

"Oh no, not in a sexual way," she was quick to point out. "I like men. A lot. But I'm contemplating cosmetic surgery." She paused for a moment, then continued. "Uh, you know, down there," she said, motioning to her crotch. "After three kids, my *area* isn't what it used to be. And I want to get an idea of what nice sexy vaginas look like."

Yeesh! The V-word. It affected me the same as someone raking his fingernails down a chalkboard. I almost think I'd rather hear the word *cunt*.

Before I could read too much into her query, she proceeded to give me some color commentary about her own genitalia that I really didn't need to hear. The kind of information that can spoil your dinner—for a lifetime!

Uneasy with her proposition, innocent as it sounded, I suggested she buy a few issues of *Playboy*, *Penthouse*, or some of the more sleazy publications. But she countered that she'd already done that and, while informative, she really wanted to see some "good ones" up close and personal.

By now it was pretty obvious that she wasn't just trying to get her kicks, because little beads of sweat were rolling down her brow. So, feeling sympathetic to her cause, I told her to sit tight—no pun intended—for a moment and left the VIP Room.

I returned a few moments later, took her by the hand, and led her back into the dressing room where a few of the other girls whom I briefed were waiting, more than happy to oblige.

One by one, Janice inspected each of the dancers' coochies—without touching them, of course—then asked a slew of questions on elasticity, sagginess, flexibility, even color.

Janice opened up to us—again, no pun intended—and explained that her sex life had been pathetic since the birth of her last child a few years ago. She said her husband complained once that she had "loosened up" considerably. And so, with his fiftieth birthday approaching, she'd decided to do a little "nip and tuck" and surprise him.

Anyway, Janice saw all the cooter she could possibly handle, and even wrote notes on a small pad to bring to her doctor. As we were all more than happy to help strengthen her relationship with her hubby, we never charged her for the info and the pudenda peep show.

About three months later, Janice *and* her husband came into the club. They were both beaming. She said that, thanks to us, her life—and her husband's—had changed dramatically. Now, they were making love at least once a day, sometimes twice! Go Janice!

Then she pulled out a photograph—what is it with me and photographs?—and showed me what her snatch had looked like before the surgery. Ugh! Thank God I hadn't seen it in living color when she came into the club the first time. It looked like the opening of an oversized piggy bank. Before I knew what was happening, she took me by the hand, led me back to the dressing room, hiked up her skirt, and said: "Look! Look!"

Okay, I felt a little funny taking a gander at some stranger's crotch, but I have to admit, I was curious. So I looked. Wouldn't you know it, her pussy looked better than mine! Needless to say, I took down her surgeon's number—just in case. But it'll be a while before I need him. My coochie is still damn nice to look at.

# 18

## The Private Dancer

*M*any people fantasize about being an exotic dancer. But it takes more than just a hot body to strut your stuff in front of the masses—and earn a living doing it. It also takes rhythm, talent, stamina, sex appeal, personality, intelligence, and a hell of a lot of nerve. Strippers come and go from the profession all the time. It's a never-ending cycle. But I give credit to those who try— and a lot of credit to those who stay.

Randall wanted to be an exotic dancer in the worst way. Sadly, he had no rhythm, no talent, an okay personality, and a body type that, had commercial casting directors been looking for a replacement, the Pillsbury Doughboy's job would have been in serious jeopardy.

But one thing Randall did have going for him was money. I mean, the guy was seriously loaded. I think he was an investment banker, some kind of well-to-do mucky-muck in the financial world.

Anyway, I was dancing for Randall in the VIP Room,

finishing up the first song, when he asked if I'd object to being a spectator. Now, I'd danced for him on two prior occasions and had seen him in the club a number of times. He was a big spender and always tipped well, but I was a little leery about what he wanted to pay me to watch him do.

Quickly, he eased my jitters by explaining that he had a fantasy about dancing for a beautiful young woman. And apparently, that fantasy could only be fulfilled by dancing in a strip club. He told me he'd hired prostitutes and danced for them in the privacy of his own home, but it just wasn't the same. The atmosphere wasn't right or something. I thought about it for a minute and, seeing as how I didn't want to stand in the way of his dreams, I stepped aside and gave him the floor.

Because I could get in trouble for allowing a customer to remove his clothing, he agreed to pay me triple what my dances usually cost him. Basically, I'd be making $75 a song for sitting on my ass. No complaints by me!

We swapped positions and he handed me a wad of bills—$5s, $10s, and $20s—so I could "tip" him during each song. And as soon as the next tune began, he began busting a move. I mean that literally. A Chippendale he was not. Chipped beef, Chips Ahoy, even Chips-n-Dip, but definitely not a Chippendale.

When this guy shook, it looked like a tub of Jello during the Northridge earthquake. When he changed direction, parts of his body were still going the other way. But through it all, I stifled my laughter, encouraged him, and even gave him pointers, all the while stuffing the bills with which he'd provided me into the mammoth-sized briefs he eventually stripped down to. Sure, his semi-nude body was not the most pleasant thing to look at and the dancers at the male clubs didn't have to worry about losing their jobs to him any time in the foreseeable future, but I had to give him credit for going for it. And trust me, he really went for it.

Two songs were all he could take before his chest was pounding like a bass drum at a heavy-metal concert and sweat was pouring off him like sea spray flying off a breaching whale. He took the duration of the next song to wipe himself down with cocktail napkins—a sight unto itself—and catch his breath. Then he got dressed and settled back to watch me dance another song for him, as if the preceding events had never taken place.

After paying me for the dances—mine and his—he thanked me for being such a good audience and promised that the next time he danced for me, he would have a few new steps in his repertoire.

Randall came back to the club many times over the next couple of months and usually picked me to dance for him in the VIP Room. Strangely, not only did he never ask to dance for me again, but he never even mentioned the time when he did. I even asked him about it on one occasion and he looked at me as if I had a third eye growing in the center of my forehead. Go figure.

# 19

# XXX Files

Strange scenarios and strip clubs go hand in hand. One of the strangest encounters I had during my topless tenure took place at a club in Florida.

It was nearing the end of my shift when a guy—average looking, nothing special—asked me to dance for him in the VIP Room. More than ready to leave, I glanced at my watch, but decided I had enough time to squeeze in a song or two—and pocket some extra green—before calling it quits for the night.

That was my first mistake.

We went into the VIP Room and, after agreeing on a price, I started dancing. I noticed that this customer wasn't watching me like the others usually did—he was *studying* me, like he was trying to look right into me, perhaps sizing me up for something. It really gave me the creeps.

I finished the song without incident and decided to quit while I was ahead—and still had mine attached. Just as I started to put my top back on, the guy nearly broke into tears, begging and pleading for me not to leave just yet. He said he needed to see more, to see if I was *her.*

What the hell? I looked at him as if he were an alien being that had just stepped out of a spaceship. Something told me it was a look he was extremely familiar with.

The guy reached into his pocket and removed a small color snapshot and a news clipping. The photo was of a young woman, mid-20s, pretty, nice figure, wearing a bikini. The newspaper clipping was a short article about a 26-year-old woman who had apparently committed suicide. The photograph in the article was the same as the one in his color snapshot.

The man told me that the girl who took her own life was his fiancée. He went on to explain that she'd been having family problems brought on by a lack of money and had considered becoming a topless dancer to earn some extra cash. Furious at the thought of his beloved "sharing" her body with other men—even if it was only with their eyes—he broke up with her and completely severed their relationship. He even took back the diamond engagement ring he'd given her. He took the ring out of his pocket to show me, then asked me to try it on—"to see if it fits."

Now, I had no intention of putting on a ring that once belonged to a woman who I now knew to be dead. Too strange for me. Plus, I still had no idea what the heck was going on and why he was telling me all of this.

That's when he lowered the boom. From what he told me, I wished Mulder and Scully were there with me—either them or an exorcist!

The guy was convinced that his ex-fiancée had come back from beyond and invaded the soul of a topless dancer. Apparently—if I took him at his word—he'd been searching for the better part of a year to find her. He said he'd been to hundreds of topless clubs across the country and though he was going broke in the process, he was certain that he'd find her one day and he wouldn't give up until he did.

At each new club, he watched—for hours, if necessary—as the dancers took their turns on stage. He scrutinized each, waiting for one of them to give him "a sign"—to call out to him in some ESP-esque non-conventional way. When that happened, he asked that girl to dance for him privately in the VIP Room, so he could study her more closely, to see if she was, in fact, *her*.

And on that day, her was me—or so he thought.

Why do I get all the weird ones?

He pushed the diamond engagement ring at me again. "Please, try it on," he pleaded. "I really think you're her."

I felt bad for the guy. I really did. He obviously had a lot of guilt over what had transpired. But I'm not a psychiatrist, I'm not a mental health worker, and I'm definitely not his deceased ex-lover. So I figured I'd try on the ring and put an end to his crazy-assed belief.

Mistake number two.

Wouldn't you know, the damn ring fit perfectly! Not okay. Not pretty good. Perfect with a capital "P." His mouth stretched in an ear-to-ear smile as tears started streaming down his cheeks. Then he hugged me as if he had known me for years—and hadn't seen me in ages.

I was scouring my brain, trying to think of a way to convince this guy that I was not who he thought I was—without hurting his feelings, in which case he might snap. But before I could come up with anything that sounded halfway decent, he broke the embrace, stepped back, and frowned.

"It's *not* you," he said somberly. "You're not her."

I was speechless. But before I knew what I was saying, I asked him why. Maybe it was my "subconscious rejection defense" kicking in. Here the guy had just let me off the hook and I was trying to jump back on! What the heck was I thinking?

But he held firm. "No," he said. "You're definitely not her." He went on to explain that he felt no "connection," no "aura" from me when we hugged. He said that when he finds her, he'll know it. As for the ring fitting—which I quickly returned to him—he chalked that up to mere coincidence.

No shit.

Without another word, he paid me and thanked me for my time, understanding, and the "possibility of hope"— whatever the hell that meant.

He left, I went home, and I never saw him again.

But I truly hope he finds *her*—if he hasn't already.

# 20

## Doc Hygiene

Everyone has a fetish, something that really gets 'em going. Those who say they don't probably have more than one, each more twisted than the next. The customers who frequent strip clubs are no exception and often they're willing to pay—in some cases, *mucho dinero*—to have their fetish fantasies fulfilled. While they may be strange (and then some!), in most cases the fetishes are completely harmless and a vast majority of the dancers (myself included) are more than willing to deliver the goods and give them what they want—provided the cash is right and no one gets hurt, bugs not included.

But that doesn't mean we aren't grossed or weirded out by some of the fetishes proposed by our all-too-eager-to-pay customers. I mean, let's face it, some of these people are just downright freaky!

One regular I'll never forget definitely made my Top Ten list of taco-short-of-a-combo-plate individuals. It was during my tenure at a Southern California club—no surprise here, as the West Coast seems to house an awful lot of nuts and wackos—that I came to know a man I nicknamed Doc Hygiene.

Tall, handsome, muscular, Doc Hygiene reminded me a lot of Tom Selleck, but with black hair and no mustache. He said he was a dentist and by the way he talked about teeth, the other dancers and I believed him.

Doc Hygiene came in once a month, always on a Friday or Saturday, regular as clockwork, and picked three or four of us to go back to the VIP Room with him. Then, he popped on a pair of thin rubber gloves and proceeded to give us each a dental check-up, one at a time, while the other girls danced.

Ironically, I was a registered dental hygienist by this time—something I never confessed to him—and I could tell by his actions that he was, indeed, a dentist. And he was very good at what he did, too. Doc Hygiene even went so far as to bring a set of dental picks, in a sterile bag, to remove any tartar build-up we'd accumulated between visits.

Now I know what you're thinking: Who in her right mind would allow some stranger claiming to be a dentist to put a bunch of foreign metal objects in her mouth in the back room of a strip joint, especially with AIDS and all the other diseases floating around these days? To that, all I can say is: He was handsome as hell, drove a new Porsche Turbo, wore a Rolex Presidential with more diamonds than they had at Tiffany's, and a few of the girls had been to his office to have cavities filled and so forth, so we trusted the guy. And thanks to his skills, the girls he selected always had the whitest cleanest teeth in the club.

So what's so weird about a friendly neighborhood dentist providing his oral-hygiene services in the back room of a strip club, you ask? Well, nothing really—unless you consider the fact that this guy would floss his own teeth with the very same pieces of dental floss he used on us!

I kid you not. After he got done flossing one of the dancers, he took that exact same piece of floss, now grimy and frayed, and ran it between his own chompers. And he repeated the procedure with each girl, using a new piece of floss for each dancer. I used to joke with some of the other girls that his antics constituted some form of oral sex.

Now, I know from my studies that the human mouth contains a truck-load of germs, a fact Doc Hygiene was undoubtedly aware of. And some of the strippers—myself *not* included—jeez, who knows what they put into their mouths? Hell, I've heard some of the things that come *out* of them and clean ain't the word for it!

But Doc Hygiene seemed to enjoy his little fetish and so long as he was paying us for our time, over and above the free check-ups and cleanings, we weren't about to complain.

However, his little perversion—harmless as it was—kept myself and the other girls at a social distance. Good-looking, wealthy, drives a Porsche ... all qualities any sane woman would want in a man. But throw in his little tooth-scraping hobby and it shouldn't be hard to imagine why none of the girls ever considered accepting one of his many invitations for drinks and dinner after work.

# 21

## Dirty Dancing

No, Patrick Swayze was not one of my customers. Ditto for Jennifer Grey. However, I have been to the Catskills—although I never danced there. At least, you can't *prove* that I danced there. Anyway, people come to strip clubs for a multitude of reasons. But not in a million years did I ever expect anyone to come looking for stripping lessons, though, while working at a club in Las Vegas, that's exactly what happened.

It was early in my shift when a young couple—early 20s, at most—strolled in and took a seat at one of the tables farthest from the stage. They struck me as a quiet bashful pair and, judging by their appearance—blue jeans and T-shirts; the guy was wearing a baseball cap—and oh-so-innocent demeanor, I guessed they were from somewhere in the Midwest.

For some reason, I found myself watching this couple. Like fish out of water, their uncomfortable body language suggested they really didn't want to be there. So, being the congenial people-person that I am, I walked over and took a seat at their table. This aggressive action shocked them at first—and obviously made them even more uncomfortable than they already were—but after I introduced myself, lit up a cigarette, and offered each of them a smoke, they settled down. Amazing what a little nicotine can do, huh?

Within a few moments, I learned that they were, in fact, from the Midwest—a small town in Kansas, to be precise. When she told me her name was Dorothy I almost peed my pants. His name was Bud.

"As in Buddy?" I asked him.

"No, Budweiser," he replied. Hops on the brain, I figured, but it seemed to suit him.

They'd been married less than 24 hours ago at one of Sin City's drive-through wedding chapels—and even paid a few extra dollars to have an Elvis impersonator in the ceremony.

When I pressed them for their reasons for visiting the strip club, they were embarrassed at first, but Dorothy—who, upon closer inspection, didn't even look old enough to *vote*, let alone drink—explained in no uncertain terms that she didn't know how to be sexy. She was hoping to learn by seeing how the girls dressed, walked, and danced.

That's when her groom proposed a better idea. He wanted me to give his new bride stripping lessons for her wedding present. (Actually, the present was for him!) I could tell by the sinking of her eyes—almost entirely into her skull—that she was less than thrilled by his suggestion. But he was convinced. When he asked me what it would cost, I tried to get the girl off the hook by hitting him with a figure that would quickly make him forget the idea.

"One hundred per song," I said, figuring this couple to be the shallow-pocket variety. "With a three-song minimum."

I figured wrong.

Bud reached into his pocket and pulled out a fistful of crumpled bills, so soiled and ratty it looked like they'd been buried in the ground behind the family farm. Then again, maybe they had. Maybe the town they came from was so small it didn't even have a bank.

"I've been saving up for this trip, honey," Bud said, giving his new wife a loving squeeze. "And this will be hard-earned money well spent." He counted out three hundred yucky bucks, pushed them across the table to me, and smiled. "Make my wife a freak," he said hungrily.

Unable to control myself, I cracked up. Dorothy did, too. After a moment, so did Bud. But the laughter didn't change the fact that young Bud still wanted me to teach his wife how to get her groove on, and his in the process. He started rubbing her neck, telling her it was what he really wanted, and after a few moments she caved in. So long as she was willing, I was game. After all, money is money. And besides, the way I saw it, I would be helping to improve their marital relations.

For dance number one, Dorothy was pathetic. She was so bad, she would've been tossed out of a strip club for the blind during Amateur Night. No matter what I did, she just couldn't seem to copy it; I think her nerves were just overpowering her. So I ordered us a round of Kamikaze shots—on Bud, of course—and waited for the liquor to do its thing.

For dance number two, the improvement was staggering. She had loosened up considerably. The booze definitely helped, but I think she was becoming more comfortable with me, as well. By the end of the song, she was actually dancing pretty well—in a rednecky sort of way. The Clampetts would have definitely invited her to their next hoe-down!

Finally, dance number three was her coming-out party. Little farm-girl Dorothy was now Dot the Slut. And judging by her wiggles and gyrations, she was loving every minute of it. Bud was beside himself. By the end of the song, he was drooling. If they hadn't rushed out when they did, I thought they might've started bumping uglies right there in the VIP Room—and Bud definitely hadn't paid me enough to witness that. Fortunately, Vegas has hotels and motels approximately every five feet. I'd be willing to bet a week's worth of tips that they hit the first place they saw.

# 22

## Mama's Boy

Everyone likes special treatment, especially the customers who go to strip clubs and spend most of their time (and money) in the VIP Room. They want something extra and they're more than willing to pay for it. Gordon was no exception, although his idea of "special treatment" bordered on the bizarre, then exceeded it.

When Gordon first started coming to the club, he seemed like a regular guy. Not particularly handsome, but certainly not ugly, he had dark hair and a cherubic face. He kind of reminded me of an older Potsie from *Happy Days*. He told me he was a foreign-car mechanic—Jaguars, I think—but his fingernails were never dirty and his hands looked way too smooth to belong to a grease monkey. He liked to drink White Russians, talk about his two kids, and watch me dance to soft music. Not once did he try to touch me inappropriately and he tipped pretty well, too. All in all, my time spent in the VIP Room with ol' Gordo was rather enjoyable. But after about two months, things started to change. I mean really change.

The first four weeks, Gordon came in only on Fridays. He was there at 9 p.m. like clockwork, always at the same table on the far side of the stage. After his second drink, he signaled to me that he was ready to go to the VIP Room, where we spent about an hour—and he dropped a couple hundred bucks. Goodbye was a polite kiss on the cheek, an extra $50 tip, and a walk to the door.

Over the next four weeks, Gordon began coming in on Saturdays, too. Now, he only had one drink before we went into the VIP Room, where we stayed for around two hours. Still, he was always a gentleman, treated me with the utmost respect, and was actually fun to talk with. My tips went up, too—$100 and sometimes $150. If this guy was really a Jaguar mechanic, the Brits must have been building piece-o-shit cars, because he always had tons of cash on him.

Gordon began coming in three days a week, starting with Thursday. Now, he skipped his precursory cocktail and we'd go straight into the VIP Room. This is when he began bringing things with him. The first week it was a baby rattle, which he shook while I danced for him. At first, I thought he was tone-deaf, because he rattled all the time, never to the beat. Another night, he brought a pacifier and sucked on it in between sips of his drinks. It was around that time he began asking me to call him "little Gordon" or "little Gordie" or "baby Gordie." The whole thing was weird and getting weirder, but the money was steady and he still treated me with respect, so I wasn't about to look a gift horse— or even a gift pony—in the mouth.

For the next month, Gordon continued his thrice-a-week routine and each time he brought a new baby toy with him. Once it was a rubber hammer that squeaked when you banged it. Another time it was a hanging mobile of colorful fish and turtles that he had me hold above him while he laid on his back and swatted at it. And one time it was a bag of small building blocks that he dumped out on the floor and assembled into little houses. He was also bringing a baby bottle with him now, into which he poured his White Russians. I thought he might have been losing his mind, but one of the other dancers, midway through her second year of medical school, believed a brain tumor was to blame.

Spankings were a major part of Gordon's next phase and I wanted no part of it. But he pulled out a wad of bills and after a considerable amount of cash-assisted begging, I agreed. However, when he dropped his drawers for one punishment, I made him pull up his underpants. No way was I laying my hand against his bare skin; his rear end was so damn hairy, the only baby he resembled was a baby Bigfoot. I was so repulsed over his wish for a bareback beating that I really tore into his hide. My smacks were so loud that two of the bouncers ran in thinking *I* was being abused. They laughed their asses off when they saw that I was the one dishing it out, although I had to give them $20 apiece to buy their silence. The boss wasn't too fond of contact between dancers and customers and this scenario certainly qualified. By the time I was finished, Gordon's butt must have felt like tenderized meat—rump roast. I'm sure he was glad I made him pull his drawers up.

In addition to the bottle, Gordon began bringing in small jars of baby food and had me feed him. The money he offered was just too good to say no. I even burped him a couple of times, but believe me, he paid for it. Watching him spit up was beyond disgusting, but the cash was keeping me in high style.

The next time Gordon came in to the club, dressed in a sweatsuit, I should have realized it was a sign of trouble. I must have been blinded by his dough not to take his new garb as a warning. He'd always dressed well—slacks and a nice shirt, blue jeans and a sport jacket, etc.—but on that day he wore the kind of easy-off sweatsuit pro basketball players wear, with the snaps going down the sides.

I was in the middle of my second dance when he stood up and ripped off his pants. My eyes nearly popped out of my head—the sonofabitch was wearing a diaper. And it wasn't even one of the new ones, you know, like Depends. His looked like some funky white sheet folded over and pinned in the front with a gigantic safety pin—the kind those oversized babies in the Saturday morning cartoons used to wear. I was about to say something to Gordon when the smell hit me. An ungodly stench! And there was absolutely no doubt in my mind what it was. Sicko Gordon had pooped in his pants.

"I'll give you five hundred bucks to change me," he said with a disgusting smile.

Speechless, I fought back the waves of vomit boiling up inside me, raced out of the VIP Room, and made a beeline to the front door. I told the bouncers—Ben and Joe, the same two guys who'd walked in on my spanking—what had gone down, literally. These guys relished every chance they got to toss someone from the club and they raced back to the VIP Room like Olympic sprinters. Unbelievably, Gordon hadn't put his sweatpants back on. He was lying on his back, holding his diapered butt off the ground, still waiting to be changed.

The bouncers grabbed him on either side, beneath the arms, and hoisted him into the air. Judging by Gordon's facial color, which instantly turned whiter than the sheet-diaper (or is that *shit*-diaper?) he was wearing, I think he now knew that the only change he'd be receiving was one of venue. Forcibly.

Ben, the larger of the two bouncers (this monster was like 6'8" and 300 pounds to Joe's *smallish* 6'2" and 250), looked Gordon dead in the eyes, like a cobra sizing up a mouse, and snarled: "Where's your cash?"

Gordon was deeply afraid. (If these guys had you hoisted up in the air, you would be, too.) "In my wallet, in the back pocket of my pants," he said fearfully.

"Take what he owes you," Ben stated emphatically. "Plus an extra fifty for each of us." He turned to Gordon, legs dangling in the air. "That's okay with you, right?" Ben said between clenched teeth. It was a statement, not a question.

Gordon gulped air. "Yeah, sure. No problem."

I took the money, put the wallet back in the pocket, and handed Gordon his pants.

"Do you want him to come back again?" Joe asked me.

I thought about it for a moment. The money was good, but this guy had obviously snapped. Who knew what he was capable of? I decided to quit while I was ahead. "No," I said. "I'm through with him."

"You heard her," Joe said icily. "Set foot in this club again and we'll *beat* the shit out of you."

Gordon kind of whimpered and hung his head, but he didn't say a word. Joe and Ben carried him off and dropped him at his car—once again, literally. Gordon heeded the warning and never came back.

# 23

# Trust Fund Kid

Some people have more money than they know what to do with. But some loaded individuals know exactly what to do with their fortunes. While working at a club in Southern California, I met a young man who embodied the expression: "You can't take it with you."

He arrived alone via stretch limo, and were it not for his driver's license and two corroborating picture IDs, he never would have been let into the club, that's how much of a baby face he had. But his IDs passed muster with the bone-crushers out front and they admitted him—but not before checking his backpack thoroughly.

Any time a customer brings a bag or package of any type, it's picked through with a fine-tooth comb, as if it belongs to an irate Arab entering a synagogue. There are a lot of freaks out there, and they try to pull all kinds of stunts. Topless clubs seem to attract their fair share, like Anna Nicole Smith attracts wealthy senior citizens. But this guy only had books, so they gave him the okay. I'm sure he tipped them, as well.

The young man went straight to the bar, ordered two bottles of Dom (personally, I prefer Bollinger or Cristal), then picked the four prettiest girls in the club. In his eyes, I was one of them. The five of us went back into the VIP Room.

This club's VIP Room had a big comfy couch and a couple of plush chairs. It was also mirrored, soundproofed, and had its own stereo. "Richie Rich" plopped himself down in the center of the couch, pulled out a gangster's roll—a fat wad of hundreds secured with a thick rubberband—and peeled off three crisp bills for each of us.

"Let me know when that runs out," he said. This cute kid with the Scott Baio smile was getting cuter by the second.

He introduced himself as Brett (never gave us a last name) and asked us to take off our tops, which we did. He took a moment to check us out and complimented each of us. Unlike most men, he actually sounded sincere. Then he removed a CD from his backpack and asked me to put it on—a mix of classical arrangements. Certainly not my first choice for dance music, but it was relaxing and a nice change from the tunes we usually boogied to. That's when we found out that we wouldn't be dancing—at least not for a couple of hours.

He invited us to sit down with him, then reached inside the backpack, taking out and distributing four books. Kat got a book on art history, Mandy on the Vietnam War, Vanessa one full of American poetry, and I one on Greek mythology.

"What are we supposed to do with these?" asked Mandy, who definitely wasn't the reading type. Unless a book had pictures in it—color ones at that—chances are she'd never pick it up. Nice to look at, she was, but Mandy had the personality of a sweat sock.

"I want you to help me study," Brett replied. "I've got

final exams coming up and if I don't pass them all and earn my degree, I'm not gonna get my inheritance."

At the mention of the word *inheritance*, we all perked up. "How much are you supposed to get?" Kat asked.

"Sixty," he said casually.

"Sixty thousand is a lot of money," I said.

Brett smiled and shook his head. "No. Sixty *million*."

The four of us almost choked on our tongues. None of us were wearing engagement rings, a fact we immediately brought to his attention. He laughed and took a sip of champagne. "If I don't pass those tests, I'll be asking *you* for money." We got a good laugh over that one, but we were all mesmerized by the number he had just rattled off. Of course, he could have been lying, but I didn't think so. He didn't strike me as the lie-for-effect type.

We were all dying to know about the specifics of his inheritance. I mean, sixty million dollars isn't exactly chump change. That's "fuck you" money: When you have that much cash, you can say "fuck you" to anyone you want.

Vanessa was the boldest of the group—with a 38-DDDD chest, what do you expect?—and she came right out and asked him. Turns out Brett dropped out of college before his junior year to pursue a career in music. But after a few months the band floundered and he got wrapped up in booze and drugs. A year and two rehabs later, he was still just spinning his wheels, expecting to be able to live off the family fortune, though how they made their money he never said. But when his grandfather passed on, he stipulated in the will that Brett couldn't touch any of it unless he completed college and got a degree—in anything, as it turns out—before his 22nd birthday. Apparently, that day was rapidly approaching, so this was, for all intents and purposes, a one-shot deal.

We spent two hours asking Brett questions from the books, from areas he had previously highlighted. He got most of them right, and when he was wrong, he was still pretty close. I bet he would have kicked ass on "Who Wants To Be A Millionaire."

The comic relief of the night was listening to Mandy pronounce the Vietnamese names and cities. Not that I could have done any better, but she was really struggling and kept cracking us up. At least she was a good sport about it.

After two hours, we took a break and gave Brett a couple of four-girl lap-dances that really straightened his toes, among other things. Before we started quizzing him again, he ordered us a feast of Chinese take-out. With all the food they delivered, he must've told them to send one of everything on the menu. The bouncers couldn't even finish the leftovers, and those guys could probably eat Iowa if they tried. They were so thankful for the free grub, they told Brett he'd never have to wait in line again and that if he needed anything in the future, just to ask them and they'd take care of it. I got the impression Brett was used to that kind of treatment. The only thing money can't buy you is poverty.

We helped Brett study for nearly another five hours. By then we were all exhausted. But when he offered to take us out to a 24-hour coffee shop for a late-night snack, we all woke up. The limo ride was fun and the conversation at the restaurant got pretty raunchy; Brett asked a lot of personal questions—in some cases too personal, I thought: how often each of us had sex, what our favorite positions were, did we like to use sex toys—but for the most part it was harmless.

Afterwards, the limo dropped us off one at a time. Vanessa (and her monstrous pair) was last, but we were pretty sure she wouldn't be going home that night. Our suspicions were confirmed the next night at work. She wouldn't give us all the details, just that it was good thing he had a big bank account.

About a month later, Brett returned to the club. No limo this time, just a beautiful black Mercedes Benz 600 SL. He'd passed all his exams—just barely on the one about the Vietnam War, no thanks to Mandy's pronunciations—and wanted to reward us each with a present. The four of us got identical pieces of jewelry—gold-heart pendants with a picture of Brett inside. The thought was sweet, but the pendant looked like it came right from Zale's—during a slashed-price sale, no less. Not only will money not buy you poverty, it also won't buy you class.

We never saw Brett again, although he called Vanessa a few times and I think they went out, but she never really talked about it. We didn't press her for information. Prostitution isn't the kind of thing strippers talk about openly and she knew the rest of us weren't into it. All she said was she had to pay for her boobs somehow.

# 24

## The Jerker

Contrary to popular belief, there are some things the majority of women who work as exotic entertainers at strip clubs won't do for money. Vanessa, of the big boobs and Brett, was an exception. Her morals were about as strong as Bill Clinton's marital commitment, perhaps a tad less. From the stories I heard—many from her own mouth—when it came to clocking dollars, she was up for just about anything.

There are all types of strip clubs out there. They range from full-tilt nudie bars, where the girls can show you anything and everything, including the orifice of their choice and anything they're smuggling inside it, to overly innocent bikini bars, where even thongs and dental-floss string bikinis are too risqué. But the majority of strip clubs fall somewhere in between. These are the ones I worked at most of the time—classier joints where dancers don't have to worry about simulating sex acts with other dancers or giving near-masturbatory performances to rake in the money. They just have to look pretty, dance erotically, and show their tits.

At these clubs, if a guy touches you for any reason, other than to hold your hand while you sit with him or something harmless to that effect, he's gone. See ya'. Bye-bye. Back in the VIP Room, you can do things to him—within reason, of course—but he still has to abide by the rules. On the other hand, every dancer has her own set of rules and they apply them as they see fit.

In regard to men touching themselves while you perform for them, that's also forbidden, at least in the clubs I worked at. However, in many clubs out there, guys can touch themselves 'til the cows come home. In some, guys sit in private rooms and put coins in a slot to raise a partition and watch a girl dance for them. In others, they sit in chairs and watch as girls model lingerie just a few feet away, with no partitions separating them. These are almost always sleazy establishments, often referred to as "jerk lounges," for obvious reasons.

During one summer evening, Vanessa decided to turn the VIP Room at our club into a jerk lounge of her own.

She was having a really bad night—in four hours I think all she'd made was $60—and was stressing for money in the worst way. She was bitching about her rent, car payment, and maxed-out credit cards to the point that the other dancers and I were ready to give her our own hard-earned cash just to shut her the hell up. Strangely, we were all kicking ass that night, but she just couldn't seem to score. Incidentally, that was how it was with Vanessa. Her boobs were so big and fake, guys were either really turned on or off by them—nothing in between. That night, Vanessa couldn't turn on a lightbulb.

Finally, a guy asked her if she wanted to go the VIP Room. He had on grubby wrinkled clothes and a multi-stained baseball cap that looked like a drain plug. I once dated a guy who liked to fish and he took me out on a

Southern California party boat one time—Vanessa's guy reminded me of one of the boat's deckhands.

No sooner had Vanessa closed the door when the guy confessed to her that he wanted to jerk off while watching her dance. Man, did he pick the right girl. Any of the other dancers—myself included—would have smacked the shit out of him. But not Vanessa. She told him sure—but he'd have to pay her $200.

The guy complained that he didn't have that kind of cash on him and if he did, he'd just go spend it on a hooker. She dropped her asking price to $150, but he said he didn't have that, either. Ditto for $100. Well, desperate as she was for money, she was not about to let some guy spank his monkey in front of her for peanuts. But then he proposed an interesting scenario: He offered to pay her $10 every time he pumped his wang.

Vanessa contemplated this and quickly determined that even if this guy were the premature ejaculator from hell, it would still take him a decent number of jacks to get his rocks off. So she agreed.

Dummy!

Vanessa began her dance and was "really working it," but the guy just stood there, arms folded across his chest, acting as if he didn't care. But as soon as her top came off, he unzipped his zipper, yanked out his semi-hard little Johnson, gave it two quick pulls, and came a split-second later.

Vanessa was horrified, the guy was satisfied, and the floor of the VIP Room was anything but dignified. While putting himself away, he produced a $20 bill with his free hand, flung it in her direction, and raced from the room, leaving Vanessa to clean up the mess.

The saddest part of the whole event: Later that night, when regaling us with her tale, Vanessa was actually proud of her ability to turn a man on, and pop him off without touching him, so quickly. If only she had a clue!

# 25

# Lickity Spit

In every club, the stage is an integral part of a dancer's strip routine. This is usually the first place customers get to see the dancers and check out the goods. A majority of the customers' selections for the VIP Room take place after the dancer has performed on stage. Most dancers have gimmicks that they use to separate themselves from the other girls and attract their VIP Room clients. It's a lot like fishing, where the best bait often catches the biggest fish. For instance, some girls are real swingers and use the stage poles as if they've had years of private lessons from Tarzan. Other girls seductively rub themselves with oils and lotions. Some girls use fingerpaints to spell out their intentions, writing all sorts of nasty notions across their bodies, and some play with whipped cream, chocolate syrup, honey, and other sweets, knowing that the best way to a man's heart—and wallet—is through his stomach.

Then there was Diamond. Diamond didn't need to bring any accessories onto the stage for her creative gimmick. She relied solely on her two best friends—and her spit.

For Diamond's 25th birthday, her ex-fiancé gave her a new lease on life. Actually two: boobs. Thanks to a platinum Visa card and a top Tinseltown plastic surgeon, in a little more than an hour, Diamond's lackluster BB-sized ta-tas became bodacious double-Ds. With her toned and tanned body, sexy tattoos on the small of her back and biceps, blonde hair and big firm boobs that stood at attention like a Marine during inspection, Diamond was a ringer for Pamela Anderson. The guys loved it.

But Diamond also played a little game that drove the men out of their skin (and pants). She filled her mouth with saliva, then slowly allowed it to trickle out. It flowed over her collagen-enhanced lower lip, streamed down her chin, and cascaded onto her breasts.

When she was on stage doing her thing, guys lined up three-deep to tip her and drink her juices. They lay on their backs at the edge of the stage, tilted their heads back, and opened their mouths wide. Diamond stood over them like a mama bird stands over her chicks during feeding time, lined up her nipples with their mouths like a big-game hunter centering a trophy animal in his rifle scope's crosshairs, and pushed her breasts down, or lifted them up, to speed or slow the flow of saliva. She teasingly criss-crossed their faces and foreheads with her mouth nectar before actually feeding them her goo. But once, while giving a private session in the VIP Room, a customer got more than he bargained for. Much more.

Diamond was chewing a piece of gum to help build up her saliva when she accidentally swallowed it and started to gag. Prior to dancing for this customer and on her break, Diamond drank a protein shake from a nearby juice bar. The shake, combined with the glass and a half of White Zinfandel she'd also consumed, came back up. She couldn't cover her mouth or pull away in time—maybe she didn't even try. Either way, the customer got a liquid meal he definitely hadn't ordered. He turned green and vomited as well, emptying the contents of his stomach, which turned out to be sushi from a business dinner. The floor of the VIP Room looked like a horror-movie special-effects-artist's leftover bin.

After thirty minutes of mopping, the room was reopened for business. As for the customer, he got a refund—and a free ginger ale. At the boss's insistence, Diamond took the rest of the night off.

# 26

## Domo Arigato

S peaking of sushi, three regulars—Japanese business
men in their late 40s—who always came in together,
hardly spoke to the girls, never once asked for lap
dances, but always tipped the dancers on stage came in one
afternoon and shocked me by asking to be taken straight to
the VIP Room. Eager to relieve them of some yen, I grabbed
two by their hands and marched the three to the back.

We reached the VIP Room and as I was about to shut
the door, two much younger Japanese men arrived. Both
were dressed to the nines in dark suits and ties—I figured
them for assistants or associates. One carried a folding table,
the other a large cardboard box.

The two younger men politely excused themselves,
brushed past me, and proceeded to set up lunch: a full-on
sushi banquet, complete with miso soup, edamame (soy-
beans), and enough raw fish to make the Pacific Ocean
take out Missing Persons ads on milk cartons. They even

had a large thermos of hot sake, from which they poured me a shot. It tasted like warm nail-polish remover. Ycchhh!

One of the older men walked over to me, produced his wallet, and said: "How much you dance one hour?" He was cute and reminded me of Mr. Miyagi from *The Karate Kid*, only he was shorter and his English was worse.

I figured I'd start high and come down if necessary. "Four hundred," I replied.

The man said something to his friends in Japanese. They nodded. He smiled, paid me what I asked for, and returned to his friends. Silly me. I should have asked for a grand!

I went to work as the men ate, their assistants catering to them like professional waiters. Strangely, not one of them bothered to look at me the entire time they were there. Not even so much as a quick peek!

They ate, conversed in Japanese, and that was it. I was dancing my ass off, moving in ways that usually brought men to their knees, but they were oblivious to my gyrations. It was like I wasn't even there.

Exactly one hour after the luncheon began, they all stood and prepared to leave. As their assistants packed up what remained of the meal, and the table, the older men walked over to me and, one by one, tucked an additional $20 bill in my g-string, giggling like little kids who'd sneaked into an R-rated movie. The last man to go, the oldest of the trio, patted me delicately on the shoulder, bowed slightly, offered his thanks in English, and that was it.

After that visit, the men came in numerous times, sitting by the stage as always. They always smiled at me and sometimes even waved, but they never went back into the VIP Room again.

# 27

# Victor's Secret

No matter how hard they try, some people just aren't cut out to follow a certain path in life. Whether due to lack of skill, lousy luck, or simple fate, sometimes wanting something, no matter how bad, just isn't enough. For instance, there are wanna-be doctors who faint at the sight of blood, wanna-be lawyers who are afraid to speak in front of crowds, wanna-be singers who are hopelessly tone-deaf, wanna-be chefs who couldn't boil water, and wanna-be prostitutes who couldn't get laid in a frat house. And then there was Victor, who wanted to design women's lingerie more than anything in his life. Sadly, he had the fashion sense of a clothing buyer for the Salvation Army.

To put it mildly, Victor couldn't create a teddy if Frederick himself walked him through the color-by-numbers steps. I mean, the guy was so inept, a moldy burlap bag with holes in it would've looked better on a woman than any of his pathetic creations. Trust me, I know. For the better part of three months, *I* was his model.

The first time I danced for Victor in the VIP Room was a routine gig: a couple of songs, a couple of drinks, some mindless banter, a decent tip, and sayonara. He never said a word about his passion for (attempting to) design sexy bedwear. I should have guessed by the way *he* was dressed—a maroon silk suit, an olive-green tank-top, and a pair of black-and-white wing-tips—that his fashion sense was severely lacking.

During his second visit he popped the question and asked if I would be amenable to modeling a "sexy new line of lingerie" that he was preparing to release the following year. I told him I'd do it, but only at the club. Originally, he wanted me to go to his house with him before or after work. Uh-uh. Not a friggin' chance. If he wanted my services, he'd pay for them during my normal work hours; taking a break from dancing to model a few teddies certainly wouldn't hurt my feet—or my bank account—one bit. But when I saw the first of his creations (*creatures* describes it more appropriately), my eyes started to water.

In a word, the teddy was freakish. The back was sky-blue velvet with criss-crossing red-rubber straps connected to a triangular front piece of clear plastic with golden grommets for attaching the connectors. At first, I thought he was joking. Unfortunately, he wasn't. Victor was dead serious about his wares and he honestly believed he could beat Victoria at her own game. (Incidentally, the guy's real name was George, but Victor seemed more appropriate for the story, given his attempted career path.)

I took the hideous garment and went into the locker room. Thankfully, it was empty. It was odd that nobody was in there—usually, one of the girls was doing *something*—but I took it as a sign that Someone up above had seen the monstrosity of this outfit and cast His pity on me.

Quickly, I stripped off my clothes and pulled on the

misfit teddy. It felt even worse than it looked, if that were even possible. Thank God I remembered to bring in my bathrobe that day, for if one of the other girls, or worse yet, one of the customers, spotted me in that get-up, I would have never heard the end of it.

I returned to the VIP Room and doffed my robe. Victor's jaw dropped and tears (I swear) began to seep from his eyes. "Oh my God," he cried. "It's even more beautiful than I imagined." He told me he knew it was going to be a sight from the very first moment he had sketched it out. Well, it was a sight all right, but I'd bet every cent I had that his definition of the word and mine were drastically different.

He circled me for almost 20 minutes, inspecting this and examining that, all the while making notes on a sketch pad that contained a colored-pencil rendering of the deformed underwear I had on. When I eventually took it off, I felt like my epidermis had been violated and the shower I took seconds after getting home was one of my most memorable in years.

A week later, Victor returned to the club with two new creations (pronounced *manifestations*). Again, both looked as if they'd been dragged from a pit of primordial ooze well before they were ready. The first was a bikini-type outfit, complete with garters, that not even Dennis Rodman would wear. It was sewn from mismatched swatches of ostrich skin, and to each of the bumps he had attached a colored plastic tip, which resembled either technicolor zits or rainbow puss-filled nipples, depending on what you were smoking at the time. The second item was another teddy, similar in design to the first piece of visual cruelty I'd donned the week prior, but this one substituted fur—faux rabbit, I think—for the clear vinyl. It didn't help to improve the appearance, although I must admit it was a hell of a lot more comfortable, aside from the rubber straps, which needed to be smoothed out.

Once again, Victor did his shark routine, circling me

like I was a piece of bloody bait, making notes on his sketch pad all the while. He also asked for my feedback, which I gave with many grains of salt—neither did I want to shatter his dreams, nor nix this easy-paying gig. In all honesty, modeling his homemade lingerie, despicable as it was, was a welcome break from the dancing. Essentially, I was getting paid just to stand there, even though I looked like a sex goddess from hell.

Over the course of our working relationship, I must have tried on close to 60 pieces. Sadly, none of them were marketable. Granted, that's just my opinion, but I couldn't see a single one of them hanging in a store or adorning the page of some catalog—unless they were looking to go out of business. I don't think that even the freakiest of hardcore punks would have donned one of those nightmarish get-ups.

My modeling sessions for Victor came to a close when he informed me during his last visit that he was moving to Pennsylvania; he'd accepted a better paying job (in the computer biz, I think) and the 3,000-mile gap would obviously make things too difficult. He said he'd have to find another model near his new home to help him (lucky her!), but that there'd always be a special place in his heart for *moi* (lucky me!). But he went on to promise that when he made it big, he'd come back to the club, whisk me away, and pamper me for the rest of my life.

Trust me, I didn't hold my breath.

In the years that followed, aside from one pair of crotchless panties rimmed with what looked like barbed-wire—a garment I refused to try on for numerous reasons—I've never seen anything in the retail marketplace that even remotely resembled one of his designs. The day I do, I'll be sure to buy a sturdy umbrella, because I know that pigs will be flying.

# 28

# Bond, James Bond

People love to pretend they're someone they're not. That holds especially true for strip club customers, who often brag about having some fanciful megabuck occupation in the hopes of convincing one or more of the dancers to go home with them—usually to a cheap motel instead of their even-cheaper residential cave. Not wanting to waste their time pursuing men with champagne tastes and beer budgets, the dancers pulled out all the stops to discern the true identities and occupations of their pursuers. From having a friend follow the guy home or playfully rummaging through his wallet (if the opportunity presented itself) to hiring a private investigator for an exhaustive background search, we were very sneaky—but the ends justified the means.

Cases in point: I danced for a civil servant who tried to pretend he was a successful defense attorney, a burger-flipper who said he was the head of a major corporation, and a petroleum-distribution technician who said he was a heart surgeon. I've also danced for countless men with oh-so-boring occupations (accountants, librarians, and telemarketers, to name a few) who did everything under the sun to convince me they lived a life of danger and adventure—Indiana Jones wannabes without the whip and fancy hat. In most cases, their facial tells were dead giveaways. I can usually spot a liar. But one guy tried to get me to believe that he was a secret agent. And I have got to tell you, the jury's still out on him.

It figures that this scenario unfolded in Southern California. In Hollywood, *everyone* is trying to make it in the film biz—even an LAPD officer who pulled me over for speeding, then gave me a signed 8x10 instead of a ticket! The Tinseltown fame contagion causes people from all walks of life to play make-believe on a daily basis, so I wasn't overly surprised when one of my VIP Room customers confided in me that he was actually a British secret agent. Of course, I didn't believe him. Granted, he looked the part: He was fairly tall, moderately handsome, and garbed in a smart-looking dark suit and expensive shoes, but his dodgy British accent, which sounded like an odd combination of Higgins from *Magnum, P.I.* and *Welcome Back Kotter*'s Vinnie Barbarino, just didn't fit the bill. Still, I played along. Hell, if he wanted to pretend he was Jesus H. Christ, so long as he paid me, I couldn't give a rat's ass. Too bad he didn't look like Sean Connery. Then he could have said he was the Queen of England and I would have played along.

The first night after a lap dance and a drink, my self-proclaimed 007 motioned for me to sit beside him. After a thorough inspection of the VIP Room—during which he claimed to be checking for bugs—he leaned in close and whispered that he was really employed by Her Majesty's Secret Service and was here on loan, collaborating with the CIA and the U.S. Secret Service in order to crack some big-time international espionage ring. Yeah, right. And I was really Imelda Marcos, devoting a warehouse-sized room in my Beverly Hills mansion solely to my shoe collection.

After that night, each time he came in to the club, which was becoming more and more frequent, we'd follow the same routine: right to the VIP Room for a drink and a lap dance, followed by a thorough bug sweep of the room and a new story. Each time, I wowed and gasped at his every word, playing the dumb little stripper girl that he obviously believed I was, all the while relieving him of as much coinage as possible. And for the record, there were no pounds sterling in his billfold—just plain old U.S. currency, crumpled fives and tens for that matter.

Money aside, his stories weren't half-bad. Ian Fleming he wasn't, but I'll bet if he ever decided to put a pen to paper and scribble some of his bullshit, he'd be able to put some food on the table.

He told me about his hand-to-hand combat training, where'd he become a master of more than a dozen different martial arts; about his intensive language training, where he'd become fluent in nine different languages and dialects; about his firearms expertise, and that he could shoot any type of pistol, submachine gun, or assault rifle on the planet with deadly accuracy; about his aviation skills, and that he had a pilot's license for nearly every kind of aircraft. He explained to me what a safe house was and that he had access to many all around the world. And he recounted his daring adventures: stealing secret documents from this place; ferrying top secret computer disks to that place; horrific tales of imprisonment and torture; spellbinding stories of assassination, and on and on and on.

Did I believe anything he said? Not a word. I wasn't born on a turnip truck.

Even when he showed me the pistol he wore in a leather concealment rig beneath his suit jacket—too small to do any real damage—I still didn't think his stories, passionate as they may have been, contained even a grain of truth.

But on his last visit, something strange happened, although it wasn't until a few weeks later that I put the occurrence into perspective. After our usual drink, dance, bug sweep, and story session, he presented me with an extra large tip and said he wouldn't be coming back for a while, and possibly never.

Hating to see a steady customer go, I pressed him for a reason. He asked if I remembered why he was in the States in the first place—the espionage ring he was helping the CIA and Secret Service to smash. It was a wild story that I wouldn't soon forget, and I told him that I did.

He then told me he'd been successful, that he alone had found the turncoat—the "mole" was what he called him—and that the head bad guy had enough power to put out a large contract on his life. He said at that very moment, numerous world-class assassins were looking for him and it was only a matter of time before they found him. He said he had to go underground to save his life.

Then, he asked—begged was more like it—if I'd be willing to go home with him that night, seeing as how he didn't know when he'd have the opportunity to be with a woman again, if ever.

This was the question I was waiting for. The scum-sucking slime. I had a feeling he was going to come up with some lame story to try and goad me into going to bed with him. But two could play that game. Rather than just shoot him down with an angry rejection, I told him that I couldn't possibly sleep with him and never see him again, because my heart would be shattered if I thought something terrible had happened to him. I said that if it was just a one-night stand he was looking for, it would have been okay, but now that I knew about his dark secret and the danger he was in, I couldn't possibly sleep with him, much as I wanted to.

Immediately, he went pale and began trying a new tactic, but I told him my mind was made up and that he'd better leave now before I broke down crying. I told him I'd grown close to him and that if he stayed any longer, I'd just fall apart thinking how much danger he was in. I kissed him gently on the cheek, bid him farewell, and ran from the room, false tears pouring from my eyes.

The moment I reached the dressing room I nearly screamed with laughter. My performance was worthy of an Oscar—I only wished there'd been a Hollywood agent in the club to see it.

Weeks passed and, true to his word, my secret-agent buddy never happened in. Maybe the bad guys had caught up with him, I thought. Yeah, right. Then, the strangest thing happened. Two guys, leg-breaker types wearing dark suits and sinister expressions, came by the club and started showing a color photograph around, asking the bartender, the other dancers, and myself if anyone had seen the man in the picture.

It was a photo of my "secret agent" client descending the ladder of a small airplane. Apparently, the bartender and the other girls didn't remember him. Then, it was my turn. I stared at the photo for a long time, trying to figure out what to do. When my mind stopped spinning, I did the only logical thing: I looked them right in their eyes and flat-out lied through my teeth, telling them I'd never seen him before in my life.

Their faces wrinkled. They asked if I was sure. Concealing my fear, I told them I was. It was another damn good acting job—but one that could have had serious consequences if I didn't pull it off, assuming the two suits were for real.

Apparently, I was convincing enough. The men thanked me for my time, took back the photo, and left without another word. I took the rest of the night off, got drunk off my ass, and went to sleep wondering exactly who the hell my Secret Agent Man really was!

# 29

## The Cheese Wiz

Big Mike, as he liked to be called, owned a small Italian deli not far away from a strip club I used to work at. Often during lunch, he came by with monster-sized combination hoagies for the bouncers and stayed for a few drinks and lap dances. Big Mike also had a weird fetish he liked to play out in the VIP Room: The guy had a passion for cheese (usually muenster, occasionally Swiss). But more than that, Mike had a certain way that he preferred to eat it. I'm just thankful he wasn't the owner of a seafood restaurant with a penchant for lobster!

You see, Big Mike liked to roll up single slices of cheese, wedge them into a dancer's butt crack, and, for lack of a better term, eat them out. The tighter a dancer's ass the better. Those dancers who could really squeeze the cheese, giving him solid resistance and making him fight for every slice, got bigger tips.

Despite my love of money, I never took Big Mike up on his offer. The idea of having some scruffy-faced deli owner—

or anyone for that matter (well, maybe not George Clooney)—feed on cheese from my cheeks was not the most appetizing of images. It didn't matter that the girls wore their g-strings during Big Mike's feeding frenzy; he could've let me wear a goddamn suit of armor and I still wouldn't have okayed it. He offered me everything from $200 cash and jewelry to free cold cuts for six months to allow the chump to chomp from my rump. And each time, I refrained from slapping him—only because he gave the bouncers free food—and simply laughed off his disgusting proposition. Had Diamond or Vanessa worked at that club, I'm sure they would've done it. Hell, Vanessa probably would have done it for a free sandwich!

But other girls didn't have a problem with Big Mike's strange obsession. At least if they did, the money factor more than made up for it. Tiffany, a pale lanky brunette whose choice of a stage name, in my opinion, was an odd one considering she looked like she came directly from a trailer park—without showering—had a Vanessa-like attitude. She was always ready and willing to make a heinie sandwich for Big Mike, and who knows what else she did with him back there in the VIP Room.

Koi, a petite Japanese girl (also strange that she took the stage name of a carp-like fish) with the largest set of natural boobs I had ever seen on any Asian girl, also had no qualms about packing cheese for Big Mike. She was paying her own way through law school, without benefit of any scholarships (or so she said), and whenever there was an opportunity to make extra money in the cheese arena, Koi was never lactose intolerant.

By now, you've probably surmised (correctly, I might add) that this particular club had a very liberal attitude when it came to interpreting the law of what was legal and what amounted to prostitution—or near prostitution. Needless to say, I didn't work there very long. The customers were

scummy, the management loathsome, and the other dancers as sleazy as they came. But I got a few good stories out of
the time I spent there, without compromising my own values and beliefs in the process, which made it all worthwhile.

# 30

## Hot Air

It was always refreshing to dance for a guy—or group of guys—who really got into the act. You know, people who could let their hair down and have a good time— within reason, of course. I hated busting my butt for bump-on-a-log types, no matter how well they tipped me. Don't get me wrong, money was an extremely important part of the strip game, but seeing a customer smile, laugh, and genu-inely enjoy himself outside the fact that he was staring at my toned and tanned nakedness was often just as reward-ing. (Okay, who am I kidding? It was a distant second!)

While working at a club in Las Vegas, I came to know a man who really understood the meaning of life. I never saw him without a smile and judging by his demeanor, he got the most out of every single second of every single day. Of course, it helped that he threw money around like it came from a Monopoly game, but why not? You can't take it with you, so you might as well go balls to the wall with it.

His name was Ryan and he claimed that he made his

living as a professional gambler. Given the fact that we were in Sin City, I'd say he was probably telling the truth. But he didn't look like a professional gambler, at least not in the stereotypical sense. He didn't wear a lot of jewelry, except for a diamond-encrusted Hublot watch that undoubtedly cost more than my car. He didn't wear flashy clothes—usually just blue jeans and a nice dress shirt. And he didn't have the telltale bloodshot eyes that looked as if he'd been staring at chips, cards, or dice for 72 hours straight. Believe me, while working in Las Vegas I met many of those types. After a while, they became easy to spot.

But Ryan did have his own eccentricities: for one, a major thing for balloons. I don't know if he used to be one of those kids' party entertainers before he made his fortune, but he sure learned his craft somewhere.

He always had a pocketful of long colorful balloons and could blow up a dozen of them in a few minutes—definitely not a smoker—and twist them into all sorts of weird animals. He made dragons, two-headed dogs, bird-fish things, and other odd creatures that not even Dr. Doolittle would have recognized.

But he didn't stop there. Oh no.

Ryan paid me to use them as props while I danced for him, and he hooted, hollered, and cheered me on every step of the way. The more I worked the balloon creature into my routine, the more excited he got—and the more he paid me. Now, I don't want you to think I was humping these balloon animals or rubbing them against my body or kissing them or anything like that. That wasn't what he wanted. If I had, I would have told him straight up to get some other chick (unless the $$$ was really ripping).

No, Ryan liked it—correction, *loved* it—when I *abused* the balloons. Punched them, kicked them, threw them against the walls, you name it. Of course, he wanted it done in a sexy way, not just full-on attacks like Mike Tyson battering Peter McNeely. He wanted to see all my usual shakes, wiggles, and gyrations, provided they were done in the context of causing the balloons harm.

And then came the big finale: the "death" of the balloon creatures. Ryan inserted $20 bills into the balloons (sometimes $50s) prior to blowing them up, thereby giving me incentive to stomp the shit out of them. The louder they popped, the louder he squealed. A couple of times I thought he might have had an orgasm. Even some of the other dancers questioned me about that after he left. When they saw the broken balloons scattered about the room, they really got curious. I tried to explain what was going on, but I honestly don't think they believed me. Hell, I didn't believe it myself and I was the one doing it. Still, weird as it was, his money was as green as the next guy's and it sure beat some drunken bum trying to put his dirty paws all over me.

One night, after some Monday Night Football game on which he apparently won a ton of money—he claimed more than $100,000—he blew up close to 50 balloons. I made more than $1,000 in 90 minutes that night, one of my biggest tallies ever, but believe me, I worked damn hard for it. My feet and legs were so tired from stomping, I took the next couple of days off and treated myself to some well-deserved pampering at a fancy Sin City hotel spa. Massages, mud baths, seaweed wraps, a pedicure and a facial—and my rent got paid, all for a single balloon safari.

After a few more visits he stopped coming in. Maybe he bet all he had on the wrong team. I wouldn't have put it past him. All I know is, I sure missed him. Despite his freaky little fetish, he was pretty cool. But I felt the absence of his money even more.

# 31

# Lounge Lizard

I love animals. Dogs, cats, birds, fish, even snakes—I danced with a python once, but that's a different story. I had quite a few snakes as customers, too, but that's a *totally* different story. To tell you the truth, I like animals better than people. The majority of them just want to be left alone to do their own thing or be loved by their owners. But despite my love for all creatures great and small, that didn't mean I wanted to *dance* for them.

At one club, a close personal friend of the owner was a rare reptile dealer. This guy, Steve, had all types of lizards and snakes and used to get bent out of shape if any of the dancers had on snake- or lizard-skin shoes or outfits when he came into the club. One time after hours, he brought in a real cobra to show the boss and actually let the thing go in the VIP Room for a little while. It had fangs, a hood, and everything. (I thought they were illegal—and should be— but I was informed otherwise.) He wanted to put a rat in there with it to show us all how it hunted its prey, but the other girls and I made the biggest fuss, saying that if he tried to feed some poor defenseless rodent to that evil serpent in our presence, we'd all quit on the spot. Needless to say, the boss made him put the snake back in its box.

Of all his creatures, Steve's favorite was an iguana, a huge five-foot-long dinosaur-looking thing named Rudolph. It had a strange dark-red blotch at the tip of its nose, so I guess the name was appropriate. Rudolph had a gold collar set with a slew of semi-precious stones that probably cost more then any of the jewelry myself and the other strippers wore. There's just no justice in the world when a cold-blooded lizard has nicer accessories than you do.

One night, Steve brought Rudolph into the club for a special occasion: his ninth birthday. The lizard wore a small glitter-covered party hat and its usual "gimme some food and leave me alone" grimace. For the festive occasion, its owner wanted to treat him to a double-girl lap dance. As luck would have it, the guy picked me and a dancer named Veronica to do the deed.

So into the VIP Room we went. Steve ordered each of us a drink—I needed a double for this gig—a vodka rocks for himself, and a Coors Light for Rudolph, which he poured into a bowl. Judging by the way the lizard lapped it up, Rudolph was no stranger to brew.

"All he drinks is Coors Light," Steve informed us, as if we really cared. "Everything else gives him nasty gas." More than enough information.

When Rudolph finished his beer—without a belch, I must add (perhaps he'd read Emily Post's rules of etiquette)—his owner set him on the couch and plopped down beside him.

"Okay," he said. "Make my lizard happy."

Veronica and I looked at one another. There are nights when all dancers wish they'd chosen a different career path. This was definitely one of them, for both of us. But Steve was a friend of the owner. Better yet, he was a paying customer, and in the topless profession, that's really all it boils down to.

So we danced for the birthday iguana, a total of three songs, and wouldn't you know, that damn lizard actually watched every move we made. Good thing he stayed on the couch, though, because if he hadn't I would've had a new pair of iguana shoes and a matching purse and belt.

However, I must admit that both Rudolph and his owner were on their best behavior. After the dances, Steve thanked us for taking him seriously and tipped us an extra $50 apiece. In the spirit of the occasion, I gave Rudolph a little peck on the top of his head—Veronica was afraid to go near him—and wished him a happy birthday, too. The ungrateful reptile didn't even bother to say thank you. That's the last time I kiss a lizard, birthday party or not.

# 32

## Bored Games

*I*'ve never been one for board games. I don't under stand chess. Checkers seems moronic. And I don't have the patience to sit through games like Monopoly or Life. I'm okay at backgammon, but there are other things I'd much rather do—like watch paint dry. But if you throw money into the equation, well now, that's a whole different story.

I'm not talking about *playing* for money, mind you. No chance I'm going to bet on something unless I have some kind of edge—hey, I worked in Vegas, remember?—but if some schlub wants to take me into the VIP Room and pay me to kick back, relax, and play him in the game of his choice instead of busting my butt dancing, where do I sign up?

And that was exactly what Ernie wanted. All that was missing from his get-up was a pocket protector and a pair of horn-rimmed glasses. I'd bet a week's worth of tips that he was the president of the computer club in high school and that his favorite movie was *Revenge of the Nerds*. He always had plenty of money, but he was extremely shy and didn't seem to relate well to people. However, he had no problem talking to me, though he never said much.

The first time he came in, he sat at the end of the bar and sipped his drink, seemingly ashamed to even glance at the girls on stage. I felt sorry for him, so I walked over and sat down beside him. I offered him a cigarette, which he refused, and I nearly finished my entire smoke before he said one word to me and that was this: "Do you like to play games?"

Immediately, my wheels began to turn. Another pervert, I figured, looking for a dancer who didn't need a dictionary to define prostitution. But against my better judgment, I asked him exactly what kind of games he had in mind.

Ernie reached inside his jacket pocket, took out a miniature folding Scrabble set with magnetic letters, and asked me if I'd play him.

I told him I'd love to—lying through my teeth, of course—but as he could plainly see, I was at the strip club because I was—guess what, peckerwood?—working. That's when he explained that he had every intention of paying me whatever I normally got to dance.

"Let me get this straight," I said, expecting someone from "Candid Camera" to pop out from behind the bar and tell me I'd just made the next episode, "You want to pay me to play you in Scrabble?"

"Uh-huh," he said. "However long it takes to play a full game, I'll pay you your normal rate."

A dream client, I thought to myself as I took him by the arm and led him to the VIP Room. After ordering some drinks, he set up the game and we picked our tiles. I began trying to formulate a word. After a few minutes, I knew there had to be someone upstairs with a sense of humor. I had a Scrabble. My word: nipples.

Can you believe that? I couldn't, but I put it down and raked in the points. I wound up kicking his ass badly that day and made $160 in the process. Ernie didn't even want to see my tits.

A few days later, Ernie came back, this time with a full chess set. Like I said previously, I know very little about the game. The horse moves in weird directions. Those little guys up front only move straight ahead. The king acts like a fairy because he can't touch anything. Forget it. But one of the other dancers was really good. Her boyfriend actually played in tournaments. Whoever says topless dancers don't like intellectual men have another thing coming—smart guys are the best, so long as they're cute and have money.

Anyway, I brought Carmen into the VIP Room with me and she absolutely destroyed poor old Ernie. Believe me he was trying, too. She beat him five games straight. In one game, I think she only made six or seven moves before she put him in checkmate.

Over the course of two months, Ernie and I played all kinds of games, including a number of different "kiddie" card games—Go Fish, War, and Concentration. Ironically, he didn't beat me once. Good thing he didn't play me in poker—he would have gotten really hammered.

I looked at my VIP Room time with Ernie as paid breaks and I was truly sorry when he stopped coming in. Still, there was something creepy about the guy I just couldn't put my finger on. I'm only glad he was a good sport and never snapped while he was in my presence. Guys like that—the quiet ones with peculiar habits—are the ones you need to watch out for.

# 33

## King For a Day

*I*'m sure you've heard about—or know of—people with a Napoleonic complex. Well, I once had a customer who had a Caesarean complex. No, he didn't have a desire to come in through the window or burrow into my belly. He simply wanted to spend a day being treated like a Roman emperor: waited on hand and foot by a slew of semi-naked lovelies, myself among them.

Now there's nothing wrong with being pampered, especially by sexy servants. I've indulged in numerous queen-for-a-day spa routines myself. But this scenario was a bit different. The "king" in question was somewhere in the vicinity of 100 years old, had more wrinkles than Willie Nelson's grandfather, was on a portable oxygen machine, and arrived in a wheelchair under the care of a full-time nurse (a sweet black lady in her mid-50s) who went everywhere he did. But this didn't stop him from renting out the VIP Room for two hours to fulfill a lifelong fantasy.

Why he waited so long, I'll never know. Even if this guy

was using Viagra or some kind of African yohimbe root or ate a couple dozen oysters or some other exotic aphrodisiac, I doubt he could have gotten a woody. If he had, his heart would probably have stopped from lack of blood flow. Although I doubt that a woody would have made his VIP Room experience more enjoyable. I mean, it's not like he was gonna get laid. But the way he sat there and drooled, it didn't even seem like he knew what was going on.

Still, we honored his requests to the best of our abilities. Four of us dressed in togas, which we eventually stripped out of, down to our g-strings, and fanned him with fake plastic palm fronds that his nurse doled out. One of the girls attempted to feed him grapes, also per his request, but he couldn't chew the skin, so she just rubbed them against his lips.

Despite his feeble appearance and condition, the old geezer had the alcohol tolerance of a career drunk. He put away two bottles of cheap red wine and was still coherent enough to direct us through our lap dances, telling us exactly how he wanted to see us move. Although some of his commands were little more than drooly mumbles, we just did what we thought he was saying and his smiley bobbing-head-doll nods clued us in that we were right on the money.

While it was obvious he was having the time of his life, I think the two hours of ecstasy—or perhaps the two bottles of wine—took their toll on the guy. With about ten minutes left on the meter, we noticed he was sound asleep. At first, I thought he might have kicked the bucket, but his nurse quelled our fears and said he was just napping. (I checked his pulse just to be sure. It was faint, but it was there.) The nurse settled his tab, added in a lousy $5 tip for each of us, and wheeled him away.

# 34

# The Tape Worm

*F*etish freaks are common in strip clubs and I met my first about a month after I started dancing. For years I'd been keeping a journal, writing in it every so often, but after this experience I began a daily log of my stripping adventures—or in some cases, misadventures. Ultimately, it was this story that spawned my book.

His name was Darren and at first glance, you'd swear he was a *GQ* model. Tall, lean, handsome, great dresser, awesome smile, perfect teeth—the guy had the full package. Somewhere in his late-30s, this was the kind of man most women would consider the catch of a lifetime. But looks can be deceiving, as I quickly found out.

After my turn on stage, Darren asked me if I would accompany him to the VIP Room. Are you kidding? For you, I'd dance for free. But as soon as we set foot inside the VIP Room, everything changed.

Darren reached inside his sport jacket and removed a small reporter's notepad, along with an expensive-looking tortoise-shell fountain pen. After writing down my name, he handed me the pad and told me to write down exactly what he said. Clueless as to what he was talking about, before I knew what was happening, he pulled out this tiny tape measure, dropped to the floor, and attempted to measure one of my feet.

I immediately stepped back and asked him what the hell he was doing. He simply told me to look in the notebook I was holding and I'd understand. So I did. It was filled with women's names, a few on each page, and below each were all sorts of numbers. No words beside the numbers, mind you, just numbers, many with fractions.

Darren was a measurement freak, an obsession I'd never even heard of up until that moment. Apparently, his mom was a work-from-home seamstress and throughout his formative years, he was her helper. Now in adulthood, his passion for measuring had taken over. He had hundreds of names in that notepad—and thousands of corresponding measurements. Who knows just how many notepads he had at home?

Still a bit weirded out by the whole scenario, I told him I didn't really feel comfortable with the game. You've got to remember this was early on in my topless tenure. Never did I expect anything like this. If I'd known then what kind of zany things were going to happen in the years to come, I probably would have become a flight attendant. If things got too freaky, you could always toss the offender out of the cabin or strap on a parachute and jump out yourself.

I told Darren the only way I'd let him measure me would be to bring some of the other dancers into the VIP Room. Safety in numbers and all that jazz. Of course, he'd have to pay us all for our time. I didn't think he'd go for it, but realizing he didn't have a choice, he reluctantly agreed.

Before I left to get some other girls, I made it extremely clear to him that there'd be no touching of my breasts or any other *sensitive* areas. I told him straight up that he'd lose his hands at the wrist if he tried. If he wanted certain measurements, the other girls would handle it—and he'd have to pay extra for those. (Remember, I was a fast learner.)

I left and came back a few moments later with Misty and Jasper. At first, they didn't believe me when I told them why I needed them, but the thought of easy money, along with their own curiosity, resulted in a high-heeled footrace back to the VIP Room.

Darren was overly pleased with the two women I had selected; Jasper played semi-pro beach volleyball and stood close to six feet tall. Sizing her up, I think his measuring tape became erect!

After introducing Darren to the girls and agreeing on the dollar amount—Misty and Jasper still didn't believe he was actually willing to pay for this strange service and insisted on cash for the equivalent of two lap dances up front—we got down to business.

Once again, Darren began with our feet. Not only did he measure the length and width of each foot, but he measured individual toes, too. When he finished with our feet, he measured the span from the ankle to the knee. Then, he went from the knee to the thigh, a measurement he should have let us handle based on our previous agreement. Before we could stop him, he put the tape to skin and brushed Jasper's nether region. Whether he did this on purpose or not was irrelevant—he paid the price big time.

Like lightning, Jasper pounded him on the top of the head as if she were making a kill shot. Darren hit the floor, more startled than injured, but I'm sure if I checked his head a few minutes later, there'd be a bump the size of a kiwi fruit.

Lifting her foot, Jasper glared at him and said something like: "Give me one good reason why I don't turn you into an orthodontist's wet dream?"

Darren swallowed hard and quickly produced a $50 bill. "This, plus my sincerest apologies."

Jasper snatched the bill before he could withdraw it, then let him off the hook with conditions. "If it happens again, your entire wallet won't be enough."

"Understood," he said. Then he recovered his measuring tape and got to his feet. "May I continue?"

I've got to hand it to him, he had guts. And we all had bills to pay, so we agreed. However, we kept him in pretty tight check. If he even got close to brushing against us inappropriately, the glares we assaulted him with sent shivers up his spine. Fortunately, none of us had to "punish" him any more that day. Good thing, too. I had just gotten my nails done and I didn't feel like breaking one.

Darren measured just about everything on the body that could be measured: fingers, fingernails, eyelashes, eyebrows, lips, even a strand of each of our hair. It takes all types and this guy was definitely one of the wackier ones. However, aside from that one incident with Jasper, there never were any other problems.

He came in at least six more times, measuring just about all the girls in the club. He even got the house mom and one of the bouncers to agree to go into his notebook. I'm not sure what he paid them, but I'll bet it was more than he paid us. What he did with all those numbers, we never knew.

# 35

# Trick or Treat

O f all the many cities I've danced in, Los Angeles has, by far, the most resident nuts, kooks, weirdos, and freaks. I'm convinced that, many years ago, a large number of mental-institution parolees got together and rented an apartment. When that apartment got too crowded, they formed a city—L.A. But I can't blame it all on Tinseltown, for my former profession tends to attract a shitload of screw-loose individuals. Ask any stripper and she'll tell you that sooner or later—in most cases, *sooner*—a weird customer with an even weirder request will happen along.

That was the case with a man I liked to call Freaky Frank. Believe me, the nickname fit him to a tee. Apparently, the guy was a hotshot in the special-effects biz. Science fiction and horror were his specialties, or so he said. (I'd never heard of any of the movies he claimed to have worked on, but I'm also not a big fan of science fiction or horror flicks.)

The first time I met Frank, he seemed like just another guy. We had a drink at the bar, I danced for him in the VIP

Room, we talked a bit, he tipped me and left. Nothing out of the ordinary. But the next time he came in, *Freaky* Frank had taken over his body.

He brought two scarier-than-hell rubber masks with him. One looked like a man who had half of his face melted away by acid, resulting in some disgusting smear of blood, flesh, and gore. The other was some kind of insect-alien thing, with many pairs of miniature claws poking out of the nostrils, above the eyes, and around the ear holes. Freaky Frank claimed to have created both and you could tell he was proud of his work. I have to admit, if they were his original creations, the guy had one hell of an imagination, though I wouldn't have wanted to get lost in his sick and twisted mind after dark. I don't even want to imagine what kind of nightmares he had, although he probably *enjoyed* them.

Anyway, Freaky Frank didn't bring in the masks just to show off his talent—he wanted me to wear them when I danced for him. Now, I've been asked to wear all kinds of things for men in the past: wedding dresses, garters, lingerie, bikinis, a chef's hat—but never a friggin' movie mask. That kind of request doesn't do a whole lot of good for a woman's psyche.

But Freaky Frank was quick to assure me that my looks had absolutely nothing to do with his request. He simply loved seeing his creations come to life and it was his deepest desire to see his mask on the body of a sexy woman, especially a topless dancer. He said he'd once asked his wife to don one of his masks before making love, but she became so furious that he had no choice but to bring his unusual request to the strip club—and straight to me. Was I lucky or what?

After a few minutes of haggling, we agreed on a price— over and above my lap-dance rate—for which I would don his mask. I honestly didn't want to mess up my hair, nor did

I want to have some disgusting latex, previously worn by god-knows-who, rubbing against my flesh, but the extra $200 would be a welcome addition on my next shopping spree.

So I pulled on the mask, did my best not to think about any cooties I might be contracting, and started to dance. Breathing was a bit difficult inside the thing and I got a little claustrophobic, but before I knew it the song was over. You better believe I had that filthy thing off my face a split-second later. That's when he handed me the alien mask. Oh no, I said, the deal was for one mask—not both. He offered me two more $100 bills to reconsider. Man, I hated being put on the spot like that, but you don't have to be a rocket scientist to figure out that $400 goes twice as far as $200, especially in the stores in Beverly Hills.

I snatched the cash, pulled on the mask, and shook my ass. As luck would have it, that song just happened to be some extended-play version—over five minutes long—but I finished the dance as promised. When I took off the mask, my face was covered with sweat. I had a new respect for horror-film actors and any performers who had to undergo intense make-up treatments before filming. How those poor people managed on *Star Trek* for so long, I haven't a clue.

Freaky Frank came back a number of times over the next few months and each time he brought some new creation with him. There was a snake-man, a living dead guy, and a humanoid robot thing, but the mask that scared me the most was the one of this woman who had eyes in the back of her head, peering out from beneath her mop of blonde hair. The mask looked exactly like one of my old high-school teachers, and my friends and I always joked that she had eyes in the back of her head, because we used to pass notes when she wrote on the blackboard and she always caught us.

Anyway, some of the other girls got in on the act of

wearing his masks—for some, it was a substantial improvement—although the amount he paid dropped considerably. One of the girls didn't know a thing about bargaining, so when she jumped at his initial offer, it lowered the bar for the rest of us. I eventually quit wearing the masks. By then the cash just wasn't worth the discomfort.

# 36

## The Abusee

Some people get off on being dominated. I used to be friendly with a customer-service rep for a major airline who moonlighted as a dominatrix. She told me all kinds of wild stories and blew me away with how much money she was pulling in. It was way more than the airline job paid, that's for sure, but unfortunately, no prime benefits package came with her whips, chains, paddles, and leather. (If there had been, I might have switched professions; I certainly didn't receive one for stripping.) The majority of her clients were affluent men in high-ranking managerial-type positions, including a number of CEOs whose incomes were well into seven figures.

While working at a strip club in Los Angeles, I had a customer who would have been perfect for my dominatrix friend, though the abuse he enjoyed was not the sort she usually dished out.

Glenn was a fairly well-known talent agent at a major agency in Hollywood. Having never been in the TV or movie biz, I had no clue who he was, but one of the other dancers recognized him immediately. She told me he represented some of the bigger names in the industry and the fact that she had worked in many movies—mostly B-films and late-night erotic cable flicks—gave me no reason to doubt her.

I was just getting ready to take my turn on stage when Glenn asked if I would accompany him to the VIP Room. I had to tell him that if he really wanted me, he'd have to wait. With a sexy wink, I said he'd be sorry if he didn't. The fish was hooked. He sat down, ordered a drink, and waited. When I was done collecting my dollar bills, I grabbed his arm and led him into the back room.

After a pair of lap dances, we talked for a little bit and I pegged him as a nice guy. Then he reached into the pocket of his sport jacket, took out a small plastic rubber dart gun—the kid's-toy type with a suction cup at one end—wet the suction cup, cocked it, handed it to me, and asked me to shoot him in the forehead. I was dumbfounded. Images of me on some dumb TV show performing stupid tricks for a nationwide audience danced through my mind, but I quickly realized that wasn't the game. No way in hell would the owner of that club allow a TV camera in his VIP Room—too much crazy shit went on back there.

"Fifty bucks," I told him.

Glenn smiled and pulled out a $100, along with a second dart. "Here," he said, stuffing the bill into my hand, "now you can shoot me twice."

So I did. With two darts now stuck to his forehead, he resembled some well-dressed insect with orange feelers. Strangely, he left them sticking there, put away the dart gun, and asked me to perform another lap dance. Midway through the dance, the darts came unstuck from his forehead and dropped onto his lap. He casually put them away and kept right on watching me. When the dance was over, he settled up his tab, gave me an extra $100 tip, and that was that.

A few days later, Glenn was back in the club and we went straight to the VIP Room. We stuck to the previous routine: a pair of lap dances and some small talk. Then, he excused himself and went to the men's room. He returned a few moments later holding a fresh roll of toilet paper, which he asked me to roll him in.

I'd been dancing for years, but being asked to turn someone into a Charmin mummy was a new one on me. Still, the $100 bill he dangled in front of me made the decision easy. Within seconds, I was trussing him with t.p. in a manner that would make an Egyptian pharoah jealous.

Glenn started coming in more often, about every three days or so. Each time, after the usual two dances, he had me perform some outlandish but harmless act of "abuse" on him. One time, he wanted me to beat him with one of those ball-and-paddle toys. Another time, he had me shoot rubber bands at him. Another time, I repeatedly snapped his fingers with a small mouse trap-like device. On one occasion, he actually asked me to give him a hot foot with a book of the club's matches, but I refused, despite the fact that he offered me $300. I just couldn't force myself to willfully burn someone. I had gone to a children's burn hospital once to read stories to the kids and I wanted nothing to do with fire and flesh.

I refused other of his requests. I wouldn't pound his feet with a rubber mallet. And I wouldn't put him in handcuffs and tickle him with a feather. I was afraid that, God forbid he had a heart attack or something while in handcuffs, the judge would throw the book at me, no matter what I said in my defense. Another time, I passed up the opportunity to shoot toothpicks at his butt from a drinking straw. It wasn't that I was against doing those things to someone I didn't really know or care about. I just didn't want to do those things to *him*. I sensed something scary about the guy and I didn't want to be the one he eventually lost it on. Maybe it was because he controlled the careers of so many people or because he was just a sick twisted fuck. I didn't know and I didn't care. I wasn't about to go against my better judgment.

The final straw came on the night Glenn asked me to pick my nose and fling boogers at him. He even offered me $500. While I'm sure some of the other girls would have done it for far less, I had to keep from losing my dinner. I left the room without even bothering to collect the money he owed me for the two dances I performed and asked the bouncers to show him the door.

That was the last time I saw Glenn in the club. Ironically, I saw him at a nice restaurant with a woman about a month later. I know he saw me, but he never said a word. Only once did I catch him looking in my direction.

Glenn and his date left about twenty minutes before my girlfriend and I got the check. Only there wasn't a check. Apparently, someone had paid our bill. The waiter informed us that he'd promised the payer he wouldn't reveal his or her identity, but I had a pretty good idea who it was. I guess Glenn felt bad for what had happened.

That night proved that you may be weird, or even seriously fucked up, but you can still have class.

# 37

# Old McDonald

*I*n the sex business, farm fetishes are nothing new. I love animals, but I also know what bestiality is. Fortunately, the one experience I had with a guy with a full-blown farm fetish was at the most harmless end of the spectrum.

His last name wasn't McDonald, and he was definitely not a farmer, unless farmers are garbing themselves in Armani these days. I figured him for an accountant or an attorney, maybe even a sports agent. Styled hair, clean-shaven, manicured nails, well-dressed … I should have also figured this guy for a weirdo. That's usually how it is. The more money a guy has, the farther he is from normal, especially in the arena of sex.

The first time he came into the club, he lavished the girls on stage with $5s and $10s. (Most people just throw $1s. Hell, some people even throw change.) During my shift on the main stage, I must have made $300 from him alone. It was a good sign of things to come. After about an hour, he picked three of us to go back into the VIP Room. Things started out normally—two of us danced while one sat with him. That went on for a few songs. Then he asked if we did any imitations. Dawn had taken some acting classes and actually had a few impersonations in her repertoire. She could do Cher, Meryl Streep, and a half-decent Joan Rivers, too—but that wasn't what he was talking about.

This wackola had a thing for chickens, goats, cows, and pigs. He'd grown up in the city and hated every second of it; his only joy was when he visited his grandparents at their farm.

This deep-seated love of the farm had apparently carried over into adulthood. Why he didn't just buy himself one I haven't a clue, for I'm pretty sure he could afford it. Judging by the way he threw money around, he probably could have bought a redneck family to run it for him, too.

He wanted us to imitate his treasured animals during our dance routines. I wasn't in the mood for a guy with a fetish. Neither was Barbi. Dawn was a different story.

First, she was flat broke. This girl had a major shopping addiction. When it came to gadgets, contrivances, and just plain stuff, she had one of everything—probably two.

Second, acting hadn't exactly paid off for her yet and she was still deep in the red from her photo shoot and 8x10s, zed cards, acting classes, and talent showcases.

Third, Dawn had moved to Los Angeles from Iowa, where her family owned and operated, you guessed it, a farm. So when the guy explained what he was looking for imitation-wise, Dawn was only too happy to oblige.

Barbi wanted no part of it and left the VIP Room. I also declined to perform, but I just had to stay and watch. Having more experience dealing with VIP Room customers, I helped her negotiate a good round figure ($600 for two songs) and she went to work, incorporating every single farm animal she could think of into her lap-dance routine.

I watched her for about 30 seconds in stunned silence before feeling queasy and getting out of there. There was just something unsettling about seeing an attractive nearly naked young woman rolling around on the floor, squealing like a pig wallowing in mud. It took a few drinks to shake the image; in truth, sometimes I still have nightmares about it.

# 38

## Human Viagra

The vast majority of the customers I danced for in the VIP Room were strong able-bodied men (both young and old) who looked as if they wanted much more from me than I was willing to give them. At the very least, they appeared healthy, alert and, well, *alive*. Pops (what he asked me to call him), on the other hand, looked like he was at Death's door. Actually, he looked as if he'd walked through Death's door and stood in the foyer for over a month!

The first time I laid eyes on Pops, I actually thought he had expired right there in the strip club. He was sitting at a small table in a dark corner and, after observing him from afar for a few minutes, I saw no sign of movement. He was propped straight up, eyes forward, hands at his sides. The problem was, the direction he was looking, nothing was happening. All the activity—the stage, and the girls on it— were far to the right. He was staring at the wall and had been for quite some time.

I was actually afraid to walk over for fear of what I might

find. Eventually, I worked up the courage. When I got to within a few feet and he still didn't move, I got really worried. But then I saw the faint rise and fall of his chest and I knew he was still alive; well, he was breathing at any rate. I nudged him. He stirred, turned his head toward me, then apologized for "nodding off."

Nodding off? Fuck! The old geezer slept with his eyes open. If that's not the creepiest thing, I don't know what is. Anyway, he asked me in a voice coarser than 12-grit sandpaper if there was anywhere we could go that was quieter. He said he'd be happy to pay for my time. Since that club had a VIP Room that was nearly soundproof, we started heading back.

This was no speedy trip. Pops moved slower than a tortoise on ether. I should have charged him for the time it took us to get back there. I would have been able to retire. During this epic journey, which was only about 40 feet, he introduced himself as Pops. In fact, that was all he said during the marathon walk. It seemed like he needed every ounce of air he could suck into his lungs. How he'd even gotten into the club was a mystery. A guy like that usually comes with a wheelchair, a bottle of oxygen, a nurse, and maybe even a priest to issue last rites just in case. I was worried he was going to code on me before I even got my top off.

Finally, we reached the VIP Room and he sunk right into the overstuffed velour couch. In the light—slightly brighter than the club's main area—Pops looked ten times worse. Man, I've seen corpses that looked better than he did. Corpses that have been buried, no less. For decades.

Anyway, after his breathing had returned to normal, he gave me the bad news: The doctors had given him only two weeks to live. Cancer, he explained. Throughout his body. Now I've heard all types of sob stories from guys who were looking to get a discount—or total freebies. But I believed Pops. Heck, if he'd have told me that he died last week, I probably would have believed that, too.

Still, he knew how to play it and he waited a few minutes for his words to sink in. Of course, I told him how sorry I was and asked him what I could do to lift his spirits. That's when he reached a shaky hand into his front pocket and pulled out a crumpled wad of bills. The bills looked so old, I swear I saw a moth fly out of them.

A count of the money revealed the sum of $19, not enough to start the music playing, let alone get a look at my bodacious ta-tas. Pops said this was all the money he had left until his next check came, but that was more than two weeks away—and he didn't expect to be around to cash it.

So, I went ahead and broke the first rule of topless dancing, the one about giving away anything for free. I turned on the stereo in the room, put on a sensual song by Prince, and gave Pops the lap dance of his life. I figured if his heart stopped while I was performing, at least he'd be checking out with a smile on his face.

When I finished the song, Pops was smiling, all right. In fact, the old codger even had a little pup tent going in his pants, a visual that embarrassed both of us. I told him I would have loved to dance for him more, but that I really had to get back to work for paying clients. He said he understood perfectly and thanked me sincerely for making his "last moments on Earth" some of the happiest of his life. I helped him off the couch and walked him back to the bar. Only now, he seemed to have a spring in his step; the journey back was made in half the time of the original trip. Hmmmm.

I got him a nice seat by the stage and told the bartender to comp him for a couple of rounds. The guy was dying. What could it hurt to be a little charitable? Then I went back to work and forgot all about him. A few hours later, I noticed he was gone. Strangely, nobody remembered seeing him go. And it wasn't like this guy would have moved at light speed.

Two weeks later to the day, Pops was back, looking as miserable as ever. I found him seated at the same dark corner table where I'd originally noticed him. In the middle of a break, I sat down and asked him how he was.

Terrible, he said, explaining that the doctors had given him another two weeks to live. I thought that was good news, but he explained that he'd already made his peace with this world and now he just wanted his suffering to end. He made it quite clear that he was ready to move on. That's when he asked me if I could give him just one more lap dance—"one more reason to smile." He even took out what little money he had left—a whopping three bucks—and said he'd gladly give it to me.

How I kept from crying, I haven't a clue. I've always been a real softy and this guy seemed as pitiful as they came. According to him he had no family, all of his friends had long since passed away, and he'd gotten so sick of sitting inside his tiny house—which didn't even have a TV—that he just had to get out.

It never occurred to me to ask Pops how it was that he managed to get his bony ass to the strip club; I was too caught up in his terminal story. So, sucker that I am, I spent the last ten minutes of my break dancing for Pops for three bucks.

Well, wouldn't you know, two weeks later old Pops was back, explaining how the doctors were all stupefied; some minor miracle must have taken place. The cancer that had ravaged his insides from head to toe was now completely gone, like it never existed. But Pops knew the true identity of this miracle cure: Me! The only catch was the doctors feared that if this cycle were interrupted, the cancer could come back in a flash and take him. Hence, I'd have to keep performing for him—for free, of course!

Now, I may have been born in the daytime, but I wasn't born yester-daytime. I resigned myself to the fact that I'd already been suckered twice by this guy; he certainly wasn't going to get the hat trick. At least not from me. With hands on hips, I tore into Pops, berating him savagely for preying on my emotions like he had. I told him I thought his actions were cruel and mean and downright sinister.

And you know what he did?

The old sonofabitch smiled, shrugged, stood up, and waltzed out like he owned the joint. Not long after afterward, I found out that he *could* have owned the joint if he wanted to. Apparently, he was one of the wealthiest men around, not to mention one of the cheapest. Getting things for free wasn't just a game for him—it was a lifelong obsession, one that he'd obviously mastered. I found out that he pulled the same routine in various strip clubs, restaurants, and bars throughout the city.

P.T. Barnum said there was a sucker born every minute. Well, as much as I hate to admit it, this one time I proved he was right.

# 39

# Ride 'em Cowboy

Every year in early December, the National Finals Rodeo comes to Las Vegas. And with it comes a truck load of tough-as-nails and handsome cowboys—along with a whole lot of money. After these guys are done busting broncs, riding bulls, and roping calves, they come out to party like madmen and blow some of their hard-earned cash. Nearly all the strippers make serious bank during the NFR, but one night, a dancer named Becky made something better than money—she made a statement.

A group of seven cowboys had been at the club for more than an hour. They drank beer like it was water and spent money like it grew on trees. Up until that point, all of their time was spent at a table beside the main stage. Now, liquored up and rarin' to go, they asked Becky and me to accompany them back to the VIP Room. Seeing that their wallets were still way too heavy, we eagerly accepted.

For the first few songs it was business as usual. They paid, we danced. A couple of them got a bit handsy at times, but it wasn't anything we couldn't handle. Then for some reason, the conversation turned to women in the rodeo—cowgirls. Turns out these seven guys were the biggest male chauvinists in Sin City—perhaps on the planet.

Now Becky is a tomboy in the truest sense of the word. She grew up with five brothers. She tried out for the boy's football team in high school at a time when girls just didn't do that, and she made the team, too, only to quit a few days after. She claimed she'd only done it to prove a point. In short, she knew how to handle herself.

Becky wasn't pretty, but she was attractive. She was tall, about 5'9" or so, and a bit on the stocky side. One of those big-boned farm girls. She was also big on top—double-Ds, all natural. But despite her size, there really wasn't much fat on her. She worked out every day, taught a few aerobics classes, and even had a black belt in judo. Straight up, the girl was tough. So when the guys started ragging on all the women in their sport, Becky got extremely defensive. That's when she made the ludicrous statement that if the guys thought they were so tough, and women were so weak, why didn't one of them try to ride her.

At first, the cowboys took her challenge as a sexual come-on, but she explained that she'd pretend she was a bull. One of them would get on her back and, if he could stay on her for the full eight seconds, just like they did in real bull riding, he'd win. She'd apologize and shut up from then on. She also thought they should bet on it—a night of free lap dances against $1,000. At first, the cowboys thought she was bluffing—and so did I—but Becky was as serious as a snakebite. She got down on all fours to prove it.

When the drunken cowboys realized she wasn't playing around, they huddled up and discussed the situation. After a few moments, one of the dudes took off his Stetson and the cowboys filled it with money until it totaled the afore-mentioned thousand. Then the biggest cowboy of the bunch came forward. His belt buckle was nearly the size of my face.

He said, "Little lady, I've ridden all sorts of creatures. But riding you is gonna be one of the greatest pleasures of my life." It sounded so corny, so affected, I'll remember it forever. And with that, he threw a leg over her back and sat down.

Becky smiled wide. "Whenever you're ready," she said. She looked at one of his buddies. "Use your watch to time it, although I don't expect it to last very long."

The cowboy on her back jabbed her with his boot heels. "We'll see about that, missy," he said.

Becky glared. I'd seen that look on her before. Once, a guy had intentionally grabbed her boob as she climbed down off the stage. She bent his wrist back so far, I thought she was going to snap it off. After he sank to his knees in obvious pain, she kicked him square in the face, knocking him out cold. Well, Becky had that look in her eyes again and I felt really sorry for the cowboy. He was in serious trouble, he just didn't know it yet.

Then the cowboy with the chronograph watch yelled: "Go."

Everything happened real quick, but it seemed like slow motion to me: The cowboy on Becky's back grabbed a fistful of her hair with his left hand, threw his right hand up in the air, and began to simulate a bull ride. Becky gritted her teeth, hunkered down, then reared up and to the side in one spectacular motion, ending the cowboy's ride in just over a second.

The cowboy flew through the air, taking a chunk of Becky's hair with him, caromed off the wall like a pinball, and dropped to the floor, dazed.

Becky was on her feet in a flash, standing over the semi-conscious cowboy, who had rolled over onto his back. "Keep the hair as a souvenir," she said before turning her back on him and snatching the cash-filled cowboy hat from one of his friends. Without losing a single bill, she flipped the Stetson up onto her head, tugged at its brim, gave the cowboys a wink, and walked out of the VIP Room. The rest of the group just stared for a long moment before going to the aid of their downed buddy. After they helped him to his feet, I took that as my cue to leave. Becky and I took the rest of the night off and went to the bar at the MGM Grand to celebrate.

# 40

## Squeeze Play

Madison was tall, blonde, and had a great body. From a distance she resembled Darryl Hannah and that's where her stage name came from. Madison was the name of the mermaid Darryl Hannah played in *Splash*.

Madison had one of the most beautiful snakes I've ever seen: Some kind of rare albino python, Burmese she said. It was this incredible combination of pale yellow and white, something you'd see in a movie. And it was big, too. Not terribly fat, maybe a little thicker than a Pringles potato chip can, but slightly longer than seven feet. Madison went on stage with the snake—its name was RJ—coiled around her body, covering her upper torso just enough to hide her breasts, so wearing a top was unnecessary. When it was time to expose her tits, she repositioned the snake and RJ always cooperated. It was a pretty cool show to watch.

At the time, Madison was dating one of the club's owners, so naturally she got favorable treatment and special privileges. On the nights she was working, she was allowed to keep RJ in a large glass tank in the third, and smallest, of the club's three VIP Rooms. This room was pretty shabby and didn't get much use, so keeping the snake in there didn't pose a problem. Madison would've preferred to keep it in the locker room, but too many of the other girls were afraid. Personally, I didn't care. RJ was very gentle and, although I'm not the biggest fan of snakes, I wasn't scared of it in the least. Most of the customers were slimier snakes than RJ.

Anyway, late one Saturday night about an hour before closing, a horrific male scream ripped through the club, loud enough to be heard above the music. I was on a break at the time, sitting at a table in the back of the club with a few other girls, enjoying a bottle of wine. The scream came from the direction of the VIP Room corridor, almost directly behind where we were seated, so naturally we ran to investigate.

The two main VIP Rooms weren't in use at that moment and the doors were open. But the door to the third VIP Room was shut. Suddenly, another scream echoed from behind the door. Then another. And another, followed by a loud THUD! The girls and I didn't know what to think. And as curious as we were, we were scared of what we would find. That's when the bouncers showed up and pulled open the door.

The room was pitch black, except for the heat lamp on top of RJ's tank—a top that was open. And RJ wasn't in the tank. The bouncers flicked on the lights and almost immediately burst into laughter.

A drunk the bartender had cut off a short while earlier was face down on the floor, the snake coiled around his legs, its jaws open and locked on one of his ass cheeks. When the bouncers realized who it was, their laughter turned to anger. Apparently, they'd tossed the guy out not long after the bartender stopped serving him. He'd obviously sneaked in through the back door, which should have been locked. (One of the busboys later admitted to forgetting to relock it after he had returned from a cigarette break; he was fired the next day.)

Anyway, drunks are more curious than little kids with books of matches, so when this guy mistakenly meandered into the small VIP Room, he couldn't leave well enough alone and his curiosity came back to bite him in the ass. Literally.

By now, Madison had gotten to the room and when she saw RJ out of his tank and wrapped around the guy, she freaked. In a flash, she was on the guy's back, pummeling him on the head and shoulders with one of her stiletto heels, accusing him of trying to steal her snake. The bouncers had a harder time pulling Madison off the drunk than RJ. But they finally got everyone—and everything—separated.

The drunk, still trembling with fear and reeking of urine (he'd peed in his pants), was threatening to sue. Despite his wobbly legs and slurred speech, he was promising legal action against the club unless he was given "tons of cash" before he left. Madison, holding and caressing RJ as if it were a delicate newborn, launched into a verbal assault against the drunk, cursing more viciously than any sailor, threatening to sue *him* for traumatizing her snake. Madison moved toward the guy; he jumped behind one of the bouncers.

After a few more snake-supporting tirades, Madison left the room. She gave the drunk a final glare before exiting, telling us she was going to take her snake for a calming walk. No sooner had she left when the drunk started in again with his threats. In a flash, the bouncer he was hiding behind spun around and clamped his hand down on the back of the guy's neck like a flesh-covered steel vise, silencing him in mid-sentence, then reminded him that he was trespassing. After all, he'd been thrown out of the club.

The matter was finally resolved by the club paying for a

taxi to take the guy home, along with $20 in cash to get the urine out of his trousers. He was told that if he ever came back, he'd be held down and *fed* to the snake. It must have worked. I never saw him again.

# 41

# Mr. Personality

To say I encountered some interesting and unusual characters during my topless career would be like saying Tommy Lee has an average-sized penis. But even if I'd entertained a billion clients over the years, I never would have forgotten Izzy. Correction, Thomas. No, make that Gregg. I mean Big Bob. Or was it Elaine? You see, the person to whom I'm referring went by *all* of those names. What's more, he/she had a distinct personality for each. No, he wasn't a member of some transsexual theater troupe, though if his multiple-personality routine was all a part of some screwball act, to hell with De Niro and Pacino, that guy should be the one winning Oscars. But I'm quite sure his "act" was the real McCoy. Still, Izzy/Thomas/Gregg/Big Bob/Elaine was always polite and respectful and his/her pockets were always deep. Besides, I'd bet a pair of my best pumps that he got more mental therapy out of a night in the strip club than a year at the funny farm.

The first time he came in, he said his name was Izzy.

Tall (in the six-foot range), late-30s or early-40s, he was average looking with an average build. In short, forgettable. He was also timid and didn't say much during my two-dance VIP Room set. He was so shy, in fact, that I even had to pry his own name out of him. The only thing about him I recognized when he came back in a few days later was his necktie. It was a rainbow of colors, imprinted with the faces of numerous types of dogs. A Chow, a Malamute, a Boston Terrier, and so many more, he looked like the PR guy for the Westminster Kennel Club Dog Show.

Anyway, once I recognize someone that I've previously met, I'm usually pretty good at recalling the name. It was a trick that helped me in the stripping biz—customers love to be remembered. However, something was weird: I remembered his hair as being straight. Now it was curly, and he wore a black Porsche-logo baseball cap. Things got weirder when he took me by the hand, kissed it, and introduced himself as Thomas. I figured it was simply a case of necktie coincidence. Though his face looked extremely familiar, I might have been tired on the previous occasion and hell, I've had stints where every customer looked the same.

So Thomas and I went back to the VIP Room and I did a pair of dances for him. After that, we sat and talked for a spell. Nice guy, very friendly, excellent conversationalist. If he'd been a little better looking, he would've been fun to date—if I'd known him *outside* the club, that is. Even though I wasn't physically attracted to him, I let him give me a peck on the cheek goodnight. He tipped me big, so he deserved it.

The very next night, just as I finished my turn on stage and was stepping down, I noticed Thomas, the man I had danced for the night before, sitting at a table by himself, drinking a beer. Naturally, I walked over, gave him a playful kiss on the cheek, and asked him if he'd like me to dance for him in the VIP Room again.

"Again?" he asked curiously.

"Just like last night," I replied.

That's when he told me that I was mistaken, that he hadn't been there the night before. He went on to say that this was the first time he'd ever been to this club. I figured he was playing some kind of game with me. Sometimes, guys are either nervous or just terrible at making conversation and play all types of silly games to make themselves seem charming or funny. After a couple of minutes of back-and-forth banter, I ruled out the game and figured he didn't want to hurt my feelings by turning down my VIP Room invitation, either because he wanted another girl to dance for him or he felt guilty for spending so much the night before. Whatever the case, when I started to leave, he asked me to sit and join him for a drink.

Now I was really confused. This was definitely the guy from last night. No question about it. Why he was saying he'd never been to the club previously, and never met me, was a total mystery. But I figured, screw it, and sat down at his table.

He introduced himself as Gregg—with two Gs, adamant about the two Gs—and said he owned a catering company. I was certain he'd told me he was in automobile sales the night before. Whoever he was or whatever he did for a living notwithstanding, we went back into the VIP Room after the drink. He stayed for three dances and gave me a decent tip when I was finished. Then I sat with him and talked as he had another drink, and he gave me another tip for the conversation before he left.

About a week passed before I saw Izzy/Thomas/Gregg again. This time he was dressed to the nines in a black suit and black turtleneck. He had on Oliver Peoples' glasses and, get this, his head was cleanly shaved. Had he been a shade better looking, he could have been a model for sure.

Anyway, he selected me and another girl, flashed a hefty

wad of cash, and paid for both of us to dance for him in the VIP Room. Five songs apiece individually, and two together. During our conversation, he made it known that he was the general manager of a popular nearby hotel, although he never said the name. But he did tell us his name—and it wasn't Gregg or Thomas or Izzy. Big Bob is what he wanted us to call him.

Being the curious person that I am, I had to bring up Gregg.

"Who?" he replied, looking at me as if I had a dick growing out of the side of my neck.

"Never mind," I said, and wondered how he got out of the straitjacket. Then, he left.

Two hours later, about an hour before closing time, Big Bob came back. Only this time, he had a full head of hair. Straight hair. The very same hair when he said his name was Izzy. And he wore the "Thomas personality" black Porsche cap. Seeing him again that night confirmed the Izzy personality. It wasn't just some exhaustion-induced memory. It was real, like all the other encounters with this freak. I started wondering if someone at the club might be playing an elaborate joke on me, but this was too weird and, to be honest, nobody at that club was that intelligent or creative.

Sure enough, "Thomas" selected me to dance for him privately in the VIP Room.

"Where have you been?" I asked him en route to the back.

"Real busy," he said. "Everyone wants a Porsche these days." He said he was finishing paperwork on all the deals he'd written that week, and that's why he got there so late.

Yeah, sure, I thought. Definitely a lobby button shy of an elevator.

Still, I did a few dances, he tipped me well, and that was that. I didn't even bother to ask him about Big Bob; I was sure he'd give me some bullshit "what are you talking about" reply. Truthfully, I was getting fed up and getting the run-around again would just make me more annoyed.

A few nights later, Izzy/Thomas/Gregg/Big Bob returned—dressed as a woman! This time the doormen knew something was afoul. It's hard not to spot a six-foot-tall man dressed as a woman wearing a wig of long jet-black hair, bright red "fuck me" lipstick, seriously ugly unshaven legs, and ultra-high heels that put him up in Kareem Abdul-Jabaar territory. The prominent Adam's apple was also a dead give-away. And if that wasn't enough, the other two cross-dressing freaks that came in with him screamed out in bold neon letters that all was not right in this guy's world.

As luck would have it, I was among the girls they selected to dance for them in the VIP Room. To their credit, they were polite and excellent tippers. I would have loved to hear their stories, but they kept their chatter pretty much to themselves, conversing while we danced for them. Too bad. I could have given them some good tips on makeup and clothing. I did, at least, get a name from him/her: Elaine.

For the next month, Izzy/Thomas/Gregg/Big Bob/Elaine came in on a fairly regular basis. I became friendly with most of the personalities—Izzy, however, remained shy and distant. There was never any mention of the "other" men or woman.

Just for the record, my "friendliness" was only in the safety of the strip club. Not a snowball's chance in hell would I have mixed with that guy anywhere else. Sure, he was always nice and respectful toward me, but there's a first time for everything. I didn't want to be around when he went off the deep end. I figured someday, he just might.

Eventually, I left that club and moved on to greener pastures. It got to be that Izzy/Thomas/Greg/Big Bob/Elaine wasn't the weirdest person there any more. In fact, it was one of the dancers, not one the customers, who went a bit mental. It was time to go and I never looked back.

# 42

## Veteran Treatment

*I*'ve always had a soft spot for soldiers—actually, all men in uniform, but soldiers especially. The way I see it, anyone who has the courage to lay his life on the line to defend his country deserves some modicum of respect. For that reason, I've always given "special" treatment to our men in the armed forces. Nothing lewd, mind you, just discounted rates on my lap-dancing services. I figure they've earned it.

As courteous as I was toward Uncle Sam's battle virgins, war veterans received even better treatment. If someone told me they'd taken part in any foreign conflict and I believed him, it was my policy to provide one lap dance for free. That should dispel the myth that all I cared about was the almighty dollar. I figured they had in some way contributed to my freedom, so I could therefore return the favor and contribute to their enjoyment. Every now and then, I gave a vet more than one free dance, but only if I really liked the guy.

One time, however, my benevolence got me into hot water. During a VIP Room lap dance, this crusty older man revealed to me that he was, in fact, a veteran. He clearly looked the part, so I told him of my policy and proceeded to give him a dance for free. When that one was completed, he said he was having a great time and told me to do a few more. Just so there wouldn't be any problems when it came time to settle the dance tab (sometimes I asked to be paid as I went, other times I let them pay at the end), I made sure he was aware that each song was going to cost him. But I said I'd give him a discount because I liked him.

He took out a handful of bills, showing me that had the means to pay, and I went to work. Three songs later, he stood up, tucked a $10 bill in my G-string, and started for the door.

I put a firm hand on his shoulder. "What's this?"

"Your payment," he replied. "I get the veteran discount, remember?"

Did this guy get his brains blown out in combat? I'd made it perfectly clear to him exactly what he was getting for free and what he was going to have to pay for. Bottom line: He owed me another $50, and that was without my tip.

"But I'm a veteran," he pleaded. "Of the Civil War!"

That rebuttal statement stopped me dead in my tracks. Now the guy was definitely older, that much was obvious. I put him in his early-70s, late-70s tops. Yes, he was crusty and a bit stooped, too, but the Civil War? Uh-uh. I saw *Forever Young* (Mel Gibson, yum!) and this guy didn't strike me as being the type to volunteer for any top-secret cryogenic experiments.

Ultimately, the manager (and one of the bouncers) had to be called, as I couldn't get this guy to cough up my dough. I hated to call in the cavalry (that's a little Civil War pun), I really did—I felt like I was tattling on my grandfather—

but he'd brought the situation upon himself. Needless to say, I got my money and he got an escort to the exit. The thing is, had he claimed to have fought for the North I would have let him slide. But when he swore allegiance to the Rebel Flag, he dug his own grave.

# 43

## All Amped Up

*H*alfway through a routine evening at the club, I was just coming down from my turn on stage when a man sitting in the front row waved me over and said he wanted to go back to the VIP Room with me.

At first glance, he looked like Willie Nelson: long un-kempt hair, scraggly beard, and a face so wrinkled, he would have made a great spokesperson for the prune industry. But as wrinkled as his skin was, his clothes—baggy paint-splat-tered jeans and a seriously faded denim jacket covered with sewn-on patches—were even more crumpled. Basically, he looked like he'd slept in them. For a year. Then I remem-bered seeing pictures of what Howard Hughes looked like during the last years of his life and I allowed that this guy could very well be a zillionaire in disguise. So I smiled, took "Howard" by the hand, and led him to the VIP Room.

During our walk to the back, I got a close look at the patches on his jacket. All but a few were military in nature, embroidered with Asian-sounding names. Some years before, I'd been to a gun show with a guy I was dating and had seen similar patches relating to the Vietnam War.

Once we reached the VIP Room, Howard plopped himself down in one of the room's comfy oversized loveseats and pulled out a huge wad of cash, held together with a rubberband. My heart skipped a beat when I saw the size of his gangster roll, but a closer look revealed it to be nothing but singles. What might have been thousands was, in all probability, no more than $100. Still, it was enough for a few dances—and one pathetic tip. I told him my per-dance price.

"No problem, girl," is how he replied, tossing me his entire thick-but-minuscule money roll. "You can have it all." Then he added: "So long as you use something of mine when you dance."

As I've explained, strippers get all kinds of requests. Everyone has his own "hot button," that special something that gets their juices flowing. For some customers, it's as simple as having a dancer use a personal item of theirs while they jiggle and shake. A bandana, a lucky charm, a hat—one guy even had me dance for him holding a picture of his kids. But before I could ask Howard exactly what item he was referring to, he pulled up the jeans of his right leg, revealing a prosthesis beginning just below the knee, removed it, and tossed it at my feet.

He smiled. I cringed. "You want me to dance with *that?*"

The skanky old codger double-pumped his eyebrows. "Actually, I want you to pretend it's a broom. You know, like witches ride. I want you to straddle it while you dance, and run around with it a little, too."

Now, I have a lot of respect for veterans, don't me wrong, but there was absolutely no way that I was going to stick that thing between my legs, not for a king's ransom and sure as shit not for the paltry sum he had to offer. So, horrified and altogether annoyed that I'd wasted my time with this weird one-legged bumpkin, I declined to use his prosthesis as a prop and told him that I was no longer interested in dancing for him at all. I think my exact words were: "We're done here!"

He threatened to sue me, claiming I was treating him unfairly because he was handicapped. Then he broke into a tirade about how poorly Vietnam veterans have been treated since they first returned to American soil. He got up and began jumping around, looking like he might topple over at any moment. Watching him hop around the room like a defective pogo stick and listening to him rant and rave, I began to feel sorry for him. I tried to placate him by picking up his wooden leg and dancing with it, holding it away from my body as if it were a waltz partner with bad body odor.

This course of action seemed to work. Howard cooled his jets, hopped back over to the couch, plopped himself down, and began to clap his hands to the beat of the music. I could swear I spotted a smile beneath that thick jungle of hair obscuring his face. In fact, he enjoyed himself so much that he discovered another hundred and sixty-some-odd dollars on his person, along with a previously opened candy bar that he generously offered to share with me. I politely declined, considering the fact it was a candy bar I'd never heard of and, to my knowledge, was no longer produced. Yeesh!

Howard came back a few more times while I worked at that club and always selected me to dance for him. Lucky me! But during his last visit, he got spit-on-himself drunk and revealed that his injury was not the result of the Vietnam War, but a bad traffic accident. In fact, he never actually served in the military at all. The jacket was just something he picked up at a thrift store a few years back.

And to think, all this time I'd been extra kind to him because I thought he had served his country proudly. Just goes to show you, you really can't judge a jerk by his cover.

# 44

## The Matchmaker

It's no secret that men love to date strippers. A lot of guys consider girls who work in the topless trade trophies of sorts. It's kind of like: "Hey, look at me, I'm dating a stripper." Of course, they'd never think of bringing a stripper home to Mom. Hell no. The consensus, pathetic as it may be, is that girls who take off their clothes for a living are only good for a couple of rolls in the hay and nothing more. We're definitely not marriage material. We're too stupid, too sleazy—you know all the reasons. If you remember, I dated a guy who felt this way. Briefly. But you know what? It's okay that men feel we're not the type to bring home to Mom, because on one occasion, Mom came to us.

It was late in the evening and I was on a break, having a drink and a smoke at the bar, chatting with the bartender, when a woman, late-40s/early-50s, wearing a spiffy gray pantsuit and a great pair of Prada shoes, took a seat two stools away from me. She ordered a Chardonnay and turned to survey the action. I couldn't help but think she looked out of place. But all types go to the topless clubs, and everyone has a reason for going. I guessed she had a thing for half-naked women, although the sizable rock she wore on her ring finger seemed to hint that she enjoyed the company of men, as well.

Curiosity aside, I shrugged off her presence and was about to go back to work when she addressed me. "Excuse me, Miss," she said politely. "Do you work here?"

I nodded and said that I did. She smiled and asked me if I was married. This caused me to giggle. I'd been asked a lot of questions during my years as a topless dancer, but whether or not I was married hadn't been one of them. I told her that I wasn't.

"Great," she said, moving to the stool beside me. "I might as well start with you." Next thing I knew she was removing a small spiral notepad from her purse, the kind reporters often carry, and a gold pen.

"What's your name and how old are you?" she asked matter-of-factly.

"Are you doing some sort of a story?" I asked, reluctant to answer any questions until I knew what was going on. Not that I had anything to hide, but reporters were always doing stories on the exotic entertainment industry and the majority of them weren't very flattering. And although she didn't look like a reporter, neither does Barbara Walters.

The woman smiled and put out her hand. "Forgive me. I'm being rude. My name is Marla and I'm looking for a wife for my son."

At this particular club, the girls were always playing pranks on one another. My first reaction was that this was just a practical joke, but the woman convinced me that it wasn't.

Apparently, her son, a handsome guy, although not really my type (she showed me a picture), had just broken up with his fiancée and was devastated. His mother, who hadn't liked the girl from the start, was convinced that one, a new love would mend his broken heart, and two, she could do a better job of finding him a mate than he could. According to Marla, her son had been "fraternizing with prissies and Daddy's little girls for far too long," a scenario for which she held herself accountable; her son had gone to an Ivy League school at her and her husband's urging. She wanted him to find a woman who "was a real go-getter, someone who wasn't afraid to get her hands dirty."

I laughed and told Marla she'd definitely come to the right place. At this particular club, there were some girls who would happily get a lot more than their hands dirty.

We shared a laugh and I agreed to answer her questions. At first, they were pretty basic: Do you know how to cook? Do you want children? What religion are you? Are you close with your parents? Do you do drugs? Do you like animals? Do you have any pets? Have you ever been arrested? Nothing that I found too objectionable.

But soon, the questions got a little racy: Do you like sex? Do you like oral sex? Do you prefer to give or receive? On a scale of 1 to 10, how would you rate your oral technique? How would you rate your performance in bed? Are you a screamer or a moaner? Where's the wildest place you've ever had sex? Do you like anal sex? Do you like to use sex toys? Do you own a vibrator or a dildo?

These were the kind of questions guys commonly traded at frat parties, not the kind you expected to hear from a woman shopping for her son's bride. Before long, they were so nasty that sailors would blush. Having reached my limit, I bowed out of the running for her son, but introduced her to a couple of girls who not only wouldn't have a problem with the explicit questions she asked, but would in all likelihood provide more information than she was asking for.

To my knowledge, none of the girls she interviewed that night made the grade. And maybe that was a good thing. I couldn't imagine having that woman as a mother-in-law.

# And Even More
# VIP Room Adventures

*B*ut it doesn't stop there. Not even close.

There was a guy who wanted me to strip for his invisible friend. An overbearing father wanted me to "dance the gay" out of his flamboyant homosexual son. A martial-arts expert was convinced I needed to be taught self-defense to protect myself from disrespectful customers. A woman described my actions in explicit detail (including things I wasn't even doing) to her blind male companion. An expectant father paid me to dance for him while his sister relayed information from the hospital via cell phone as his wife was giving birth. A trio of women, once in the VIP Room, revealed they were nuns and began berating me for selling my soul to Satan. A proud father tried to sneak his recently bar mitvah'd son into the club so that he could finish "becoming a man." A masochist wanted all of his back hair yanked out with tweezers. A group of guys played a high-stakes dice game while two other girls and I danced for them. And some guys celebrating a bachelor party sponsored their own version of the Olympics, rating the girls with numbers drawn on cocktail napkins after each lap dance.

Never a dull moment in the VIP Room. And these moments are happening even now, in strip clubs all over the world, if not beyond. The myriad situations—and individuals—encountered are all part of the strip club experience, which I would describe as a five-course meal for the senses. Regardless of how long you stay, and how much money you spend, strip clubs are clearly the entertainment bargain of a lifetime.

# Afterword

*A*fter seven years as a topless dancer, I was more than a little burned out. Sure, I'd taken vacations along the way, but as anyone who works in the sex business will tell you, until you decide to get all the way out, you're still all the way in. Some girls bust out within a few months of getting into the profession, while others are still going strong after 20 years. For me, three quarters of a decade was my limit, and I knew it, so I decided to say goodbye.

Beyond simple burn-out, there were other reasons behind my withdrawal from the exotic entertainment industry. For one, I found myself drinking and smoking more than I wanted to. For another, I was getting tired of the constant drama and the endless nightlife scene. I was also sick of keeping a vampire's hours. Physically, I'd reached my limit, as well. My body was beginning to shows signs of wear and tear—especially my knees and lower back. Years of dancing in high heels can wreck even the sturdiest of physiques.

But perhaps most importantly, I simply wanted to move

on with my life. Stripping had been good to me (great to me, actually) while it lasted, and I wanted to remember it as such—not go on to have regrets about staying in the game too long. Sure, there were days when I missed the fast money and the wild interactions, but whenever I needed a quick fix, I'd just crack open one of the many journals I kept during my dancing days and relive some of the memories.

And speaking of memories, the vast majority were positive. Granted, at times I was truly disgusted by the situations I found myself in, but never once did I stoop so low as to compromise my own values and beliefs. My decision to go for it not only helped me to overcome the debilitating effect of poor self-image—in all candor, an ongoing process—but it helped me in the financial arena, as well. I treated myself to new clothes, went on some great trips, bought a new car, and paid off all of my student loans. My degree in dental hygiene led to a rewarding career in the field and, as I'd already begun working during the time I was still dancing, I'm willing to bet I was one of the few stripping hygienists on the planet.

I will always hold in high esteem the women who take off their clothes for money, regardless of their reasons and personal issues. Topless dancing is hard work. Anyone who believes otherwise should try it for a night, let alone a week, a month, or a year. As a society, we tend to dismiss strippers as sluts and sleazes while we elevate celebrity actresses who take off their clothes in R-rated movies to near deity status. In my opinion, the only real difference is that strippers get paid a whole lot less.

Since I stopped dancing, I've only been to strip clubs a couple of times. I smiled watching the women running the show and laughed watching the men act like little kids in a candy store. My time in the business gave me a deep insight into men—what they want and, perhaps more important, what lengths they're willing to go to get it. My own social transition took awhile, but I eventually stopped viewing the opposite sex as little more than dollar signs. I like the company of a good man as much as the next girl.

If there's a moral to this story, it's simply this: Especially if you go to strip clubs, but even if you don't, be kind to strippers. After all, I'm quite sure you would like them to be kind to you.

## About the Author

After seven years in the topless trade, Lacey Lane permanently retired her g-string. Now she divides her time between the serenity of Scottsdale and the insanity of Los Angeles.

## About Huntington Press

Huntington Press is a specialty publisher of Las Vegas- and gambling-related books and periodicals. Contact:

Huntington Press
3687 South Procyon Avenue
Las Vegas, Nevada 89103
702-252-0655
www.huntingtonpress.com